AS A DEER YEARNS
FOR RUNNING STREAMS

Also by Lisa Di Vita:

Shattered Peacock: A Story of Life and Revolution in Iran

LISA DI VITA

AS A DEER YEARNS FOR RUNNING STREAMS

The Story of Queen Margaret of Scotland

BOOK ONE

Library of Congress Cataloging-in-Publication Data is available upon request.

ISBN: 978-1-54398-277-0 (print)
ISBN: 978-1-54398-278-7 (eBook)

Printed in the United States of America

First printed in 2019

Cover tile of "Medieval Deer" by Mary Philpott.

FIRST EDITION

For CHUCK and STEPHEN

As a deer yearns for running streams,
So I yearn for you, my God.

—Psalm 42:1
Catholic Online Bible

CONTENTS

With gratitude to the National Library of Scotland in Edinburgh, for my research time there, and with boundless affection for the months spent researching at the Huntington Library and Gardens in San Marino, California.

Special thanks to
CHRISTOPHER ADDÉ at the Huntington Library.

ACKNOWLEDGEMENTS

*T*HERE'S the research and then there are the people, the team of strong minds and loving hearts, who look at your material and give you their honest opinion. I list these generous souls in alphabetical order, because it's impossible to rank their unique abilities.

JIM BLACKFORD, a writer, a former teacher and one of the smartest, most entertaining people I know, picked up his teacher's red pencil again to contribute insightful analysis. He's a colorful writer, making me want to write like him. His help was invaluable, and I bless him for the "-ships," he offers me, both the friend-ship and scholar-ship.

NINA TRASOFF JILG and I go back many years, too many to want to add them up. Suffice it to say that the water that has flowed under the bridge is a flood. Happily, her life experiences as a television news anchor, documentarian, city council person and head of a public relations company lend her a singular perspective on writing. She's swift and incisive. Gratitude to her on so many levels.

SUSAN APPLING JOHNSON, pure and simple, is the best-read person I know. I was honored to have her peruse my manuscript. Her literacy has given her formidable analytical prowess. My favorite moments were when she'd call, laughing, to read aloud something incongruous I'd written. By the time she'd complete her rendition of my detour, I'd be doubled over with laughter, too. She possesses a wicked clarity and thankfully, has a delightful way of imparting it.

And finally, thank you to artist _MARY PHILPOTT_, who graciously agreed to let me use images of her tiles for all three of the Queen Margaret books. Her style, combining a medieval sensibility in French and English colors, with a William Morris flair and the nature-centric peace of the Arts and Crafts Movement, captures an appreciation for animals that was everything I wanted for my book covers. More of her exquisite work can be seen at verdanttileco.com.

— LISA DI VITA

INTRODUCTION

*T*HE eleventh century, an age sometimes known as "dark," for dearth of the written word, nonetheless includes two momentous historic events: the Norman Conquest of 1066 and to a slightly lesser extent, the East-West Schism of the Catholic Church.

To these events I add the birth of Margaret, Saint and Queen of Scotland, the subject of this book. Margaret's life bears examination for historical reasons deeper than her legendary beauty: one being the impact her family had on the Norman Conquest of 1066, and two, the lineage of leaders she left behind upon her death in 1093.

Outside of the United Kingdom and perhaps Hungary, people are more familiar with Scotland's Mary, Queen of Scots, she of the 16th-century, than of Queen Margaret. Interestingly, Mary was a great admirer of Queen Margaret, to the extent of keeping her head at her bedside for good luck during childbirth, since Margaret successfully delivered eight children at a time when infant mortality soared as high as thirty percent. While Mary's devotion to Margaret's head feels macabre to us, it's just one example of how Margaret influenced history.

For me, researching Margaret of Wessex for nearly a year, first in Edinburgh at the National Library of Scotland and then in San Marino, California at the Huntington Library, Art Collections and Botanical Gardens, has been a joyful scavenger hunt, comprised of searching for details to the political, religious, and social forces that molded Margaret's life, as well as the expectations placed on her and the privileges she enjoyed. I've striven to utilize the facts I gleaned by weaving them into an authentically-based, plausible, yet entertaining story.

Margaret was an exceptional woman who began her life in Hungary, where her father, Edward, was living in exile from England. Edward was an *aetheling*, meaning one who is eligible for the throne. At the time of Margaret's birth, the nation of Hungary was only about fifty years a Christian country, with (Saint) King Stephen, (István in Hungarian), having used the point of his sword to make it thus. While the fervor of evangelization still bloomed in the country, it co-existed with local pantheism and paganism, for the blood of the Magyars still flowed through the veins of Hungarians. Growing up in a Hungarian society, Margaret necessarily was influenced by a belief in magic and the superstitions of the time, even though she was raised a staunch Roman Catholic.

It's true that the eleventh century was an era of illiteracy in general, but Margaret's noble status afforded her an excellent classical education. She grew into a woman who excelled at living a model life as defined by her times. She was gentle on the outside and a force of nature on the inside, but she bent boundaries without breaking them. She took the generality of "goodness," refined it and forged it into specific ways to bless the poor. She was unafraid of a male-dominated Church. As an adult, she corresponded with high-ranking churchmen; however, although we have a couple of letters written to her, we have no extant letters written by her. The lack of her end of the conversation leaves a large hole in the puzzle. Were the powers of her writing subtle or forceful? We use the thin clues we possess to make suppositions.

Little original to the 11th century remains for us to look at. I've stood twice before the Bayeux Tapestry, stitched shortly after the Norman Conquest, thinking I was seeing the most authentic remnant of history from that century, only to learn that scholars now believe it was reworked and altered over the ensuing years. And so, despite all the scholarly research done by the very educated before me, those upon whose work I lean, certain portions of Margaret's persona remain elusive.

The genius of Margaret of Wessex included surviving historic tumult during the first part of her life, and then turning the tables to influence history during the second part of her life, an achievement made more impressive because she was not an outlier, but one who lived within the context of her time. She overcame obstacles with grace to bring kindness to a warring society and mitigated the violence in the man she married. It's fair to say that Scotland would be a different country had Margaret not existed, for even beyond her personal accomplishments, she molded Scotland for generations, not at the point of a sword, but through the children she birthed and raised, and the males among those progeny who ruled the country she loved.

— *LISA DI VITA*

REAL-LIFE PERSONAGES IN THIS BOOK, IN GENERAL ORDER OF APPEARANCE:

MARGARET OF ESSEX: The eldest daughter of Edward the Exile and Agatha. Margaret was recognized for her beauty, gentleness and piety, even as a child. She became Queen Margaret of Scotland and shortly after her death, was declared a saint.

EDWARD THE EXILE AND AGATHA: After his brother, Edmund's death, Edward became England's sole remaining Anglo-Saxon heir from the House of Wessex, an "aetheling," meaning one eligible for the throne. The throne was occupied at the time by his half-uncle, Edward, known as the Confessor. Agatha's familial roots remain unclear, but the two met and married at Kiev's Grand Prince Yaraslov's court. Edward and Agatha's union produced three children: Margaret, (later Saint and Queen of Scotland), Cristina and Edgar.

MALCOLM III, KING OF SCOTS: Malcolm III's great grandfather, Malcolm II, became King of Scots in 1005. His grandson, Duncan, was Malcolm III's father and Malcolm II's choice to succeed him; however, Duncan was killed by Macbeth. Malcolm III fled to England at the age of ten. In 1055, assisted by King Edward the Confessor, Malcolm's forces killed Macbeth. In 1057, Malcolm killed Macbeth's successor, Lulach, and was crowned King of

Scots. He married Margaret of Wessex, his second wife, shortly thereafter. They had eight children.

EDMUND IRONSIDE, KING OF ENGLAND AND EALDGYTH: Grandparents of Margaret and her siblings, and parents to the exiled princes, Edward (Margaret's father) and his older brother, Edmund.

CNUT THE GREAT, SUCCESSOR TO EDMUND IRONSIDE: The Danish King Cnut and Edmund Ironside briefly co-ruled England, before Edmund was murdered. King Cnut and Queen Emma then exiled Ironside's babies, Edward and Edmund, placing a "death by proxy" on them to avoid having the offspring's blood on their hands. They assumed the boys would be killed in Denmark or Sweden.

EARL WALGAR: This Danish Earl stepped in to spirit the infants Edward and Edmund to safety and out of King Cnut's grasp, thus saving them from certain death.

KING ANDREW (ANDRÁS) OF HUNGARY: Also known as Andrew the Catholic and Andrew the White, he ruled Hungary from 1046–1060. Andrew became friends with Margaret's father, Edward, at Yaroslav's court in Kiev. Yaroslav, Grand Prince of Rus', gave his daughter, Anastasia, in marriage to Andrew. They had one son, Salomon.

BISHOP EALDRED OF WORCESTER: An ambitious and military-minded man of the cloth, Ealdred wielded considerable influence over King Edward the Confessor. With a proclivity for collecting bishoprics, Ealdred sometimes held multiple positions simultaneously. At one time or another he was: a monk at Winchester,

Abbot of Tavistock Abbey, Bishop of Worcester, administrator of the Diocese of Hereford, and archbishop of York. He was the first English bishop to make a pilgrimage to Jerusalem. A wealthy man, Ealdred heightened his influence by lavishing churches and monasteries with gifts as well as funding their building projects.

ABBOT ALWYN: A traveling assistant to Bishop Ealdred, Alwyn accompanied him to Hungary in the process of bring Edward the Exile back to England.

YAROSLAV, GRAND PRINCE OF RUS', ALSO KNOWN AS YAROSLAV THE WISE: Ruler during the golden age of Kievan Rus', Yaroslav was a devout and learned man who sheltered several sets of exiled princes, including Edward and Edmund, perhaps with an eye to extending his influence in Western Europe. He was loyal to Rome. His spouse and consort, Ingegerd Olafsdotter, lent his court a distinctively Swedish influence.

KING SAINT STEPHEN OF HUNGARY AND GISELA OF BAVARIA: King Saint Stephen (István in Hungarian), made Hungary a Christian nation, thus becoming its first Christian King. A ruthless defender of the faith, when he suspected his cousin and potential rival, Vasul, of being a pagan, he punished him by gouging out his eyes before filling his ears with molten lead. After Vasul's death, King István set his sister's son, Peter Orseolo, on the throne. Vasul's sons, András, (Andrew), Béla, and Levente, were immediately exiled and landed in Yaroslav's court, where they met Ironside's exiled sons, Edward and Edmund. Andrew and Edward became close friends. Edward and Edmund eventually fought alongside Andrew to set him on the throne of Hungary.

King Stephen is also known for a book he purportedly wrote to his son, Emeric, who later was killed in a hunting accident. Entitled "Admonitions," the book outlines the qualities necessary to be a good Christian and leader.

KING SAINT EDWARD THE CONFESSOR AND QUEEN EDYTH: A pious, if uneven ruler, it is speculated that Edward and his wife, Edyth of Wessex, never consummated their marriage. At the very least, they were unable to conceive. Edward was widely admired for his piety. In his later years, people claimed he could heal. Edward built and is buried in, Westminster Abbey. He was a distant cousin to William the Conqueror and half-uncle to Edward the Exile. Queen Edyth, Edward's wife, was the daughter of the powerful Earl Godwin. Her family background made her the wealthiest woman in England. Nearly twenty years King Edward's junior, she treated him more like an affectionate daughter than a wife, dressing him beautifully and taking good care of him. She preferred to sit at his feet rather than next to him on the throne. Eventually, she became more powerful than he. She is shown on the Bayeux Tapestry tenderly washing her husband's feet as he lays dying.

AELFRIC, ABBOT OF EYNSHAM: While Aelfric is mentioned but once in this book, his homilies are a powerful resource, if the reader is curious. Born approximately in 955 and dying around 1020, Aelfric was a prolific and extremely literate Anglo-Saxon writer. His homilies can be found at Gutenberg.org.

HENRY IV, HOLY ROMAN EMPEROR: When Henry IV was crowned King of the Germans and Holy Roman Emperor in 1056, he was all of six years old. Yet, with his mother acting as regent, he quickly became embroiled in the Investiture Controversy, during which the Church declared that secular rulers could not make religious appointments. During the hostilities, which continued for decades, Henry deposed Pope Gregory VII and in turn was excommunicated five times.

GODWIN, EARL OF WESSEX: England's most powerful baron, Godwin first came to power under King Cnut. Three of his sons Sweyn, Tostig and Harold were also earls and became Edward the Confessor's brothers-in-law in 1045, when Earl Godwin engineered the marriage of his daughter, Edyth, to the Confessor. In 1051, the Godwin angered the king and he banished the men from England, while confining his wife, Edyth, to a nearby nunnery. When the family returned to England the following year with military forces and the popular support of the people, Edward had no choice but to restore the family to power and return their land to them.

HAROLD GODWINSON: The eldest and most powerful son of Earl Godwin, he succeeded his father as Earl of Wessex and cultivated his influence in King Edward's court. He was, as he said, "Duke by the grace of God." As Edward aged, Harold became the man behind the throne. Godwinson, who briefly wore the crown of England, attempted to thwart William the Conqueror's invasion at the Battle of Hastings in 1066.

POSTLUDE

1058 A.D.

THE COURT OF EDWARD THE CONFESSOR, WINCHESTER, ENGLAND

New opening line? ✓

QUEEN Edyth, wife of England's King Edward the Confessor, glided through Winchester Castle's great hall with recently turned thirteen-year-old Margaret of Wessex in tow.

"Certain experiences change your entire destiny," she said, "and attending Wilton Abbey is one of those experiences."

Margaret could think of some other events that had changed her destiny, but she enjoyed hearing the queen's breezy observations because she made life sound uncomplicated.

"Does Winchester feel like home to you?" asked Edyth.

"It does, my queen, because of your love. You make it home."

"You are the daughter I didn't have. You've filled an aching hole in my heart. But how is your mother?"

"The same, I fear."

"I'm sorry to hear that. I never see her in court. Change shatters some people. She may still recover. Perhaps the joy of

Advent and Christmas, so splendidly celebrated here, will lift her spirits. I certainly couldn't let you miss the holy days here."

Margaret loved Edyth but felt guilty that the deep relationship she'd developed with the queen filled the void created when Agatha, her real mother, sequestered herself away from the English court.

On the other hand, it was precisely because of the extraordinary attention Queen Edyth lavished on Margaret that she'd been set apart from the other Wilton girls. Edyth was Wilton's main patroness, a member of the powerful Godwin family, and the wealthiest woman in England. Truly, Queen Edyth had changed Margaret's life more than Wilton ever could. Their relationship made the other girls jealous, but it also secured for Margaret an untouchable level of respect, although her stoutly naïve heart took no pride it. She assumed the other girls were kind to her simply because they were good Christians.

"Christmas is much more cheerful than Lent and Easter, wouldn't you say? Let's find Edward. He will want to know that you've arrived safely. Did you put together your own outfit?"

Margaret looked down at her clothes in a panic.

"Am I inappropriate? I can change quickly."

"Never question your taste in clothing, dear one. You dressed beautifully even a year ago when you were still a country girl. Your eye for fashion is extraordinary, although I notice that these days you dress more like an Anglo-Saxon than a child of Hungary."

"The fabrics here are rich and the styles more elegant."

"That's the Norman influence. You know Edward's fondness for everything Norman and I see that you, too, have fallen under its spell."

"I still love Hungary. I just don't miss it as much as I thought I would. It's wonderful here in England. There's so much that interests me."

"That's your Anglo-Saxon blood. One's blood will always out – just like Edward's Norman blood from his mother. That and the decades he spent in exile there. Destiny is destiny. Oh, I hear him talking. He's in here."

She waved to the guard to let them in. He bowed and opened the massive door to the king's chambers. Margaret watched Edyth's demeanor change from assertive to deferential, as though she were greeting a sweet uncle rather than her husband. It was a touching subjugation of pride. Edyth bowed low to the king. But she could barely contain the excitement in her voice.

"Edward, look who's come home from Wilton."

King Edward, commonly called the Confessor for his piety, was leaning across the table, deep in conversation with another man. The king had aged some since Margaret had last seen him. She hoped he wasn't ill. She'd heard that he had healed several people recently, including a blind man, demonstrating his blessed piety, and she had been amazed to hear that despite his frail appearance, he still went hawking every day.

She stood quietly before him, waiting until he looked up at her to curtsey. His face broke into a wide smile when he saw her.

"Margaret, welcome home. I trust you've been studying hard at Wilton. Tell me what you're reading."

"St. Augustine's 'The City of God.'"

"And what languages are you studying?"

"Latin, English and French."

King Edward's visitor finally looked up, irritated by the interruption. Malcolm III was a burly man in his mid-thirties, with a warrior's bearing, but when he saw Margaret, his brain turned to "apple mush," as Edyth would later say.

Margaret did present a dramatic first impression. She was tall and slim, with chiseled features, alabaster skin and light hair. Malcolm stared at her blue eyes until she was forced to look down. She thought the embarrassing silence would never end. Edyth found Malcolm's onset of awkwardness funny, and she filled the void with polite chatter, her bemusement evident only in her twinkling eyes.

"Congratulations to you, Malcolm, King of Scots, and well-done. I've heard grand news of your coronation. And now, may I please present to you Margaret of Wessex?"

He nodded without blinking.

"Well, Edward, you two were deep in conversation when we interrupted you, and for that I apologize," said Edyth, "for it seems Malcolm has now lost his concentration."

In truth, Malcolm couldn't put together two words of conversation while Margaret was in the room. Edward was as tickled as his wife was, because he could see that Malcolm's hands were trembling. Malcolm's reaction would become their private joke.

Edyth smiled graciously.

"Your Highness, my dear husband," she said with a deep curtsey, "I just wanted you to see how well Wilton agrees with our Margaret."

"That it does," said Edward. He looked at Margaret questioningly. "But I understand that Cristina has stayed behind at the abbey."

Margaret replied, "She prefers to be there now. My little sister is changing. She's much less interested in boys now."

"Indeed, you've changed as well, Margaret. You've grown up since I saw you last."

He turned toward his guest with a gesture inviting him to engage Margaret in conversation, but Malcolm's tongue remained paralyzed, so shrugging his shoulders, Edward continued.

"Margaret, your brother Edgar returns later today. He's spent the last two months at Oxford, studying language. His greater abilities, though, lie in martial training. As his lessons continue, he shows good promise. I was going to pair him with Malcolm here, to strengthen his aggression, but it appears as though the new King of Scots has lost his first battle and surrenders to a fair young woman, wouldn't you say, Edyth?"

"Yes, my king," said Edyth, "it seems that way."

Malcolm was unaware of the world around him. He saw only Margaret.

Margaret just wanted to leave.

Once the women left the room, Malcolm quickly found his tongue. He spoke with concern to the king.

"Does she understand the danger she and her family face?"

"I'm sure she doesn't."

"She needs protection."

"Are you offering? I can't force her to do anything."

"As one king to another, promise her to me, Edward, when the time is right."

"Yes, if possible, I promise her to you. You will take good care of her, yes?"

"That wouldn't be distasteful."

On the other hand, the conversation between the two women went differently. Once the door closed behind them, Margaret turned to Edyth, flabbergasted.

"Malcolm is a very intense man. But can he speak, or is he a mute?"

Queen Edyth laughed in the silvery tone that was taught at Wilton. She'd been a student there, too, before becoming its patroness.

"That, my dear, is Malcolm III, King of Scots. He was crowned on the Stone of Scone in April. He'll be good for the northern people – a little rough-hewn, but a mighty leader. Edward and I know him well. His father, Duncan, was slain by Macbeth when Malcolm was a young lad, and he had to flee Scotland for England. He lived with us for years until he was old enough to avenge his father's death. But you know what living in exile is like."

"So do you."

"Oh, I've forgiven Edward, and so have my father and brothers. Edward has a temper, you know, and he didn't understand what my father was doing. I prefer to think of the dispute as a misunderstanding. But my family, as you know, is very popular with the people, so I was confident we'd be back sooner or later. Really, how can I be bitter, when Edward sequestered me at a nunnery, where it was peaceful, and the nuns were kind? Anyway, the Godwins are long back in his good graces, and I have my land back. But my heart hurts for poor Malcolm, for while he now has his crown, he's bereft of his wife. Ingioborg died not long ago, and so he sits alone on a cold throne. I do believe you have healed his heart without even trying, my dear. You might consider him as a husband. He's a good man."

"Oh, no, Your Highness, the Scots are like the Magyars – at least so I hear - with the wildness of the winds still ruling their hearts. No, my life is here in England, at Wilton. And then I'll become a nun."

Edyth sighed.

"Then for now, we won't speak of it. Edward and I promised you an education, and you shall have it. We shan't break our promise." She stopped and took Margaret's hands in hers. Her voice was gentle, but her message was clear. "But my dearest child, hold this one thing in your heart: King Malcolm III will leave his fingerprints on history's parchment. You'll see."

CHAPTER ONE:

Margaret's Stream

THE PREVIOUS YEAR: 1057 A.D.

LATE JANUARY

MECSEKNÁDASD (MEANING REEDY WATER), SOUTHERN HUNGARY

ETWEEN the Linden trees, near the banks of a stream, knelt an eleven-year-old girl, praying with the intensity of a monk, her eyes closed, and her hands pressed gently together as though caressing her prayers. Her honey-colored hair was the only thing unkempt about her. It tumbled down her back in disarray, giving her angelic look a touch of whimsy. She'd been praying like this for hours, her zeal sustaining her through the discomfort of kneeling on the ground. For Margaret, the forest was a living cathedral. She was in a prayerful state, so deep in joy, she was unaware that her knees were sinking into the mud. In her mind, she was attending a heavenly Mass. The song of the water flowing over rocks was her cantor, and the birds were her choir.

Unfortunately, Margaret had completely forgotten that today was an important day and she wasn't supposed to be praying

~~by the stream.~~ She was supposed to be at the castle for the arrival of an English embassy, one having traveled to Hungary from Winchester. She would never have willfully disobeyed, but she had no recollection of those instructions. Nor was she aware of the clouds gathering overhead or the large beetle crawling across her leg before falling off and scuttling beneath a pile of leaves. She felt only peace.

Not far away were Margaret's friend Ludmila, a sturdy fifteen-year-old lay sister from nearby Pécsvárad Abbey, and Margaret's tutor, Nyék, whose face was wrinkled as a prune and his legs so bowed that a pig could trot between them. They'd been tasked with finding Margaret and bringing her back to Castle Réka. Even though they hurried through the forest, they found time to disagree about something, as they always did and, as always, Nyék started it.

"I think Margaret prays too much, don't you?"

Whenever he was fretting, the tutor verbalized his anxiety loudly and relentlessly, and he was worried about finding Margaret, so he was continuously talking. He threw his head back and yelled.

"Margaret, where are you? You've forgotten your promise!"

His voice sliced through the forest air, momentarily shocking the birds into silence.

Ludmila wiggled a finger in her ear and checked it for blood.

"What are you, a rutting elk? There's no need to yell. We'll find her."

Nyék repeated himself.

"I just think Margaret prays too much," he said, throwing the comment over his shoulder, for Ludmila was trailing a few steps behind him. Her short-and-squat frame compared to Nyék's tall-and-thin one made it difficult for her to keep up with him, despite her youth.

"No, I don't think she prays too much. Aren't we told to 'pray without ceasing?'"

Nyék snorted.

"But where does it say the praying has to be done in the forest, and most favorably by a stream?"

"But Nyék, she prays for you daily. She told me."

He grunted, but Ludmila could tell the idea pleased him. Then he panicked again.

"But what if we don't find her soon enough?"

His voice cracked at the thought.

Approaching from the other side of the stream were three soldiers. The taller young one broke a stick in half and poked his buddy. The soldier and his friend were accompanied by an older, battle-weary archer named Unwin. The taller young man toted a large jug of ale. The three had sneaked away from the English embassy to drink ale in private and to hunt small game. They knew they were hunting illegally in Edward the Exile's forest, but what Edward didn't know wouldn't hurt him. Or them, as long as he didn't find out.

"A couple of rabbits. Who should care," slurred the tall soldier with the jug, taking another gulp and passing it to his buddy.

"And if someone notices, what can they say, unless it's Bishop Ealdred who sees us?"

"Ealdred better not find out," said Unwin. "That would be unpleasant."

The young men were pleased to be on an adventure with a legendary soldier like Unwin, even if he did drink too much. They didn't think their *thegn* could be upset with them. They'd just tell him they'd been learning how to track game with Unwin.

"It's going to rain," said Unwin, sniffing the air. "Let's hurry and bag a few small animals and get back to the castle. If the bishop does notice we're gone, I'll get some ungodly penance from him, just for spite. I hear a stream. Let's see if anything is taking a drink of water."

Unwin headed toward the sound. He was the first one to see Margaret praying by the stream. He stopped as though he'd seen a vision. She was so delicate; he decided his eyes were playing tricks on him. He held back the other two with his arm while he stared, trying to decide if she were real. A rush of holiness swept through his heart, quickly replaced by something akin to carnal desire, even though he tried to brush the urge away because she seemed young, not that that had ever stopped him in the past. He finally motioned for the other two to take a look, shushing them, lest she discover their presence. All three were inebriated enough to decide they'd have fun with this little angel.

"You, Bones," shouted the tall young soldier.

Margaret jumped. She'd been so deep in prayer that at the sound of a human voice, she wasn't sure where she was. Now her heart raced as she saw three strange men emerging from the trees. She struggled to her feet. They were drunk and she was all alone.

Pray for me, Saint Benedict, she pleaded silently.

"Look at you, skinny servant girl," said Unwin. "Don't they feed you, Insect? Don't worry, I have some special meat in my pants for you, my dear."

Margaret couldn't decipher his English, but his crudeness was self-evident. Leering required no translation.

Unwin spewed garlicky laughter. His teeth, worn down from eating gritty, granite-milled bread were uncomfortably close to her face. His leathered skin was pock-marked by disease and scarred from battles. She inhaled the stink from his horse-sweat soaked tunic, layered with weeks of unbathed body odor, and stale piss. She was scared. Vomit rose in her throat.

The shorter young soldier took another swig of ale.

"She's a pretty enough blossom. Give her two more years and she'll be a ripe pear. Who'll take the first bite of her?"

Margaret was fighting back panic. She tried to pray. She'd heard about what drunk men did to young girls.

"I'll have a bite," said the taller one. "Look at those eyes, blue as Lake Ullswater. Oh, yes, I'll stick my big toe into her waters."

Margaret tried to bolt past them, but they blocked her way. Unwin draped an arm around her.

"What's your name, Weed?"

"In the name of Jesus, let me pass," Margaret yelled as commandingly as she could.

The men laughed and joked in Anglo-Saxon.

The sounds reached Nyék and Ludmila: both the panic in Margaret's voice and the lewd cadences of the men. They looked at each other and ran toward the voices. Ludmila hiked up her woolen habit above her knees so she could run freely. Nothing would stop her from saving her friend.

Nyék was disoriented with fear.

"What if they're bandits? Or armed soldiers? What will we do?"

"I'll crush them by sitting on them if I have to," said Ludmila.

Her grim determination convinced Nyék that she'd make something work. She did have the bulk.

They couldn't translate the language of the soldiers, but Nyék recognized the language as the two ran side-by-side.

"They're Anglo-Saxons, but with strange accents. And they're very drunk."

"Very drunk," said Ludmila. "We have to surprise them and to make them think more people are coming right behind us."

"Agreed. You do it," he said, but immediately tried on his own to buy Margaret some time. "We're all coming to save you, Margaret! There are lots and lots of us."

Ludmila rolled her eyes. That hadn't helped.

Nyék's creaky voice only made the soldiers laugh.

The tall one said, "Is your grandfather hobbling over to save you, girl? He's going to drop dead before he gets here."

The shorter one joined in.

"Grandfather! We have your little virgin. Do you think she'll still be a virgin by the time you hobble over here?"

Margaret found courage in the fact that at least someone was coming. She squared her shoulders and proclaimed, "I am Margaret of Wessex, daughter of Edward and Agatha."

"The hell you are," said the tall soldier.

Unwin studied her.

"We may have made a mistake, boys."

"She's lying."

"No, look at her hands. They're too soft to have ever done work, and they never will."

He backed away from her. At that moment, Ludmila and Nyék burst into the clearing and began flailing at the men, who laughed as they swatted the two flies attacking them, except for the short young soldier, who ran directly into Ludmila's fist, breaking his nose. He dropped to the ground in pain, moaning.

"Run, Margaret, hurry," shouted Ludmila, who kept up her assault.

Margaret took off for the castle, her shoes a blur as she leapt from rock to rock across the stream to safety.

"There's more of us coming," said Ludmila. "Don't think it's just us, you mad men."

"Listen," said Unwin. "Be quiet. Someone is coming."

Horses were approaching. Ludmila thought fast to force the advantage.

"Well, isn't that what I just said? Those are our forces, coming to protect the royal child, Margaret."

Unwin knew they were in trouble either way.

"We'd best make ourselves scarce. A cup to a jug says that it's Ealdred's men and they're looking for us. Take different directions. Go!"

By the time the English horsemen arrived, they found only Ludmila and Nyék sitting on some rocks and shaking in fear. Unwin's *thegn* headed the group, sent by Bishop Ealdred to find the three men.

"Several of our soldiers are missing. Have you seen them?"

"Oh, yes," said Ludmila. "They were here."

"Did they have Edward the Exile's daughter with them?"

"They did, but she got away and is running back to the castle."

"Did they harm her in any way?"

"They didn't have the time. One of them has a bloody nose, though. Ha!"

Ignoring poor Nyék and Ludmila, the soldiers rode off to find Unwin and his friends. The two were left alone by the stream.

Ludmila finally stood up and brushed herself off.

"Well, here we are. We did our duty and more. Margaret is safe. It's back to the castle for us. Come, my friend, you and I need to make our way back."

She took his arm to help steady him as they walked out of the woods together.

CHAPTER TWO:

Castle Réka

MARGARET'S legs were churning so fast they might have made butter. She flew through the woods toward the castle. She was gasping for breath by the time she clambered up the rise with a view of their castle, that crowned the mound across the valley. To her right was the mining pit, and to her left lay their quaint village with water mills dotting the stream. She checked over her shoulder to make certain the men hadn't followed her. Now that she was in sight of the castle, she felt safe. But she was shocked at the scene that was unfolding below her and riveted in disbelief at the level of activity; more than two hundred men and nearly as many horses milled about in front of Castle Réka.

Then she remembered. Her heart sank. Oh, no. She'd been told to stay at the castle because the Englishman, Bishop Ealdred and his embassy were arriving today with some important news. She buried her head in her hands. In forgetting to stay home, she'd been disobedient. Surely the Lord had sent those awful men as punishment. At least He'd spared her the worst. What if they'd ripped her virginity from her? How could she properly thank the Lord for His mercy? Or ask for His forgiveness? He obviously was angry with her. She yearned for His forbearance.

Obviously, those men were part of Bishop Ealdred's retinue. That's why they were speaking English. Her stomach turned just reliving the incident. No man had ever talked to her like that, let alone touched her. She trembled at the danger she'd been in. But now, she reminded herself, she was home and nothing more could happen, except for the intimidating mass of humanity invading the castle.

The glut of people would be demanding of the Castle Réka's resources. Even though all castles and monasteries hosted guests, she'd never heard of them arriving in these numbers, not in her lifetime and certainly not here in Hungary, a country which, according to her father, barely existed to much of the world. He said he liked it that way. He must be upset, she concluded, by this invasion as well. Naturally, he wanted her home. How could she have forgotten? She wanted more than anything to please her father. She'd have to tell him how sorry she was.

She rested her hands on her walnut-shaped knees, waiting for her racing heart to slow, while trying to count the number of women sprinkled in among the men. But there were many more men than women: lords and other nobles, knights in trousered chain mail, as well as monks, friars, and clerics in dark-hued robes. Peasants in brightly-colored wool tunics were tending to livestock while others unloaded ornate chests from wagons. Pitched off to one side of the massing arose a splendid tent with colorful banners snapping in the late afternoon wind - Bishop Ealdred's field tent, she assumed.

A fat drop plopped on her shoulder. It was raining. She'd be soaked before she made it back home. After the fright she'd just experienced, though, rain didn't seem to matter so much.

A large column of people and horses were still approaching. Where did it end? She knew they couldn't all be staying at Castle Réka, and she felt sorry for the village people of Mecseknádasd and the nearby Pécsvárad Abbey, where the precisely ordered days of the nuns and monks would be disrupted and their food supply drained, as they extended the requisite hospitality.

Margaret raked her fingers through her hair, unconsciously tugging at its wet snarls. She'd have to walk past the crowd to enter the castle, and the stench of horse manure had already reached her nose, carried on the wind. Crouching low, she skirted around the backside of the large tent while praying for Jesus to carry her invisibly past the throng.

The tent flap flew open and a meticulously dressed man of commanding bearing strode out. Margaret instantly knew that she was meeting Bishop Ealdred, himself. Few men carried themselves with this kind of authority, the kind that was nurtured by the giving of orders, not taking them. She curtsied. He seemed to know who she was.

"Did my men frighten you, Margaret of Wessex? We found them hiding in the forest."

She wouldn't give them that satisfaction.

"Of course not, Your Excellency."

"What were you doing out in the forest alone? Did you think that was a safe thing to do? Or a smart one?"

He was blaming her, heaping shame onto the yoke of guilt she already wore.

"No, I guess it's not. It's just that I ..."

"Unwin come here!"

The edge in the bishop's voice could have sliced iron.

Around the corner came the oldest of the three soldiers, very sober by now.

"Unwin, why is it that wherever there's trouble, you're in the thick of it? If you weren't our finest crossbowman, I wouldn't have brought you along. You've insulted the grandchild of our martyred King Edmund Ironside."

Unwin looked chagrined. Margaret speculated that he was more upset at being caught than for his actual transgressions.

"You will volunteer to stand watch tonight. And I'll hear your confession tomorrow at *Hora Prima*, so you'd best curb your drinking; there's double penance for you if you come to me at dawn with bleary eyes."

Unwin slunk away, squinting at Margaret, as though all this had been her fault. She felt threatened by him all over again.

The bishop beckoned for Margaret to follow him inside the tent and out of the rain. A deacon and a clerk bent over a proclamation being written in Latin, its elegant letters flowing across a large sheet of parchment.

Margaret curtsied and attempted her English again. "Thank you to … come and … say something at us," she stammered to the bishop. "I know you … holy. I be … when Benedictine."

The corners of the normally humorless bishop's mouth floated upwards. "Don't worry, your reputation precedes you, Margaret. You pray alone by streams and keep visitors waiting."

She blushed. "I, sorry … be … close to the Lord …"

"As a man of the cloth, I believe that the Trinity lives indoors as well as outdoors." He paused and changed languages. "But meet Jesus where you will."

Margaret looked up, wide-eyed at his words, which she understood.

"Yes, I speak some Hungarian," he said. "A nun, you say?"

"Next year I will move into the convent."

The bishop looked vaguely into the distance, searching for the answer to an unspoken question. He sighed.

"Destiny disagrees with our hearts many times during our lives; however, we remain consoled by His promise of eternal salvation." In Anglo-Saxon he added, "And in the meantime, we make things go our way when we can." He cleared his throat. "Now go, put on clean clothes and pull a comb through that bird's nest on your head. You're a soggy mess."

She hurried across the bridge spanning the moat, between Castle Réka's timbered guard towers, and ran through its heavy doors into the safety of the courtyard's walls, where dinner preparations proceeded at a hectic clip. A cook bracing a large basket of pears against her hip didn't even break stride when she saw Margaret. She smiled, waved and spread the news.

"She's back!"

A barrel-chested man with a load of firewood relayed the news in the opposite direction. Quicker than a flying arrow, the castle walls echoed with news of Margaret's delinquent return. Horrified, she ran up the narrow, winding stairs to the household's wing of the castle, nearly knocking over an elderly lady-in-waiting.

"I'm so sorry! So sorry!" Margaret said, grabbing the woman's arm to steady her.

Eight-year-old Cristina overheard the ruckus and stepped into the hallway wearing her new outfit and a triumphant smile. Usually, she was the one who got in trouble. Margaret seemed to do everything right, but not today. Today was a rare chance for Cristina to gloat.

"Ha! You're in trouble! Edgar and I are ready, and you look a mess!"

Etel, Edgar's harried nursemaid, flew around the corner, clucking and perusing Margaret before saying, "Aren't we bedraggled? Honestly, Margaret, do you think the Lord is pleased that you make our lives difficult? I've had warm water poured into the basin. No time for a bath now but go wash your hands and face. And wipe your teeth. Into the bedroom with you. You've a new gown to wear tonight. But first we must comb out those horrid tangles. You're soaking wet! Cristina, tell your mother that your sister is home. Run, Cristina!" She turned around. "I see you there, Edgar!" The five-year-old had an infectious giggle that always revealed his hiding places. "Silly boy. You honk like a goose. Alright, Lord Goose, you stay right where you are, before you get into trouble like your sister."

Embarrassed by her mistake and her tardy arrival, Margaret decided not to mention her frightful experience in the forest. She untied her knee garters, letting the hose fall around her ankles. She laid them on the bed, trying unsuccessfully to hide their muddied knees. Etel pursed her lips but said nothing.

After splashing water on her face and scrubbing the dirt from her hands, Margaret wiped each tooth with the rough linen towel and chewed on the mint leaves that had been left to freshen her breath. Undressing, she pulled on a new pair of hose, securing them with soft wool strips.

Etel slipped a shift of fine linen, dyed in yellow weed, over her head, noticing for the first time that the girl's chest had sprouted two bumps. Oh dear, she thought, if she only knew what lay ahead of her. She wasn't going to like it.

Margaret stood still as a statue as Etel layered her shift with a long gown of imported silk, dyed sky blue in leaves from the *woad*, its sleeves embroidered five inches wide with copper stitching. The gown spilled to the stone floor like a stream, just as Etel had intended. She tied it at the waist with a sash. She would ensure that these Englishman marveled at the girl's beauty – her eyes, her hair, her delicate white skin – clear evidence of her royal Anglo-Saxon heritage and a bold announcement of her eligibility.

The nursemaid grabbed the double ivory comb with the carved handle, the one with widely spaced teeth on one side and fine teeth on the other. Margaret cringed, knowing what was coming. Etel wielded the comb like a weapon, thus the children had dubbed it, "The Comb of Death," because they wanted to die whenever she used it. The nanny yanked at Margaret's wet tangles until they surrendered to her attack. Margaret gritted her teeth and tears ran down her face, but she accepted the pain as part of her penance. After achieving submission from Margaret's hair, Etel divided it into three smooth sections, and plucking a blue ribbon from her pocket, wove it into a cheerful, if damp, braid.

Feeling better, Margaret rummaged through her trunk for her yellow felt shoes. They were like wearing sunshine on her feet, but she hesitated when she saw her mother standing in the doorway. Agatha was a strict parent, distressed by her daughter's wanderings, but even she found it impossible to be angry with Margaret for long. No girl tried harder to be good than she did. Today was just a mistake.

"Chin up, my darling. Glorious festivities await us. Don't the sucking pigs smell delicious? I can smell the cloves from here. I'm told we're serving four or five kinds of meat at tonight's feast for the bishop."

Edgar bounced with excitement.

"What, mother? What will we eat tonight?"

"The boiled beef with be served with pomegranate seeds and bitter orange slices, the fried fish is flavored with pepper and ginger and let me see, yes, I've ordered a swan for each table. Oh, and the whitest, softest bread is being baked right now - big round loaves. They will go well with the suckling pigs, I'm sure. Each guest gets their own. Oh, yes, I shouldn't forget the mutton. Would you rather have hedgehog? There's more, but I can't remember - you'll have a chance to try it all, Edgar, dear. This is a very important night for your father. Bishop Ealdred has come representing your great-uncle, King Edward the Confessor. I'll make certain you meet the bishop at the banquet. Remember, he'll take whatever is said here straight to the throne."

Margaret piped up without thinking.

"I've already met Bishop Ealdred."

A surprised Agatha frowned. That shouldn't have happened yet. Did Margaret know something that they didn't? Like what news the bishop had come to share?

Edward, her husband, stuck his head into the room before she could ask. Margaret's joy at seeing her father wilted in the heat of her guilt.

She whispered, "Hello, Father."

"Margaret, you look lovely. Let me see those eyes. Oh, no, don't look gloomy."

"Please forgive me, I'm sorry I went to the stream to pray," said Margaret, a tear dropping onto the floor. "I forgot." She didn't want to tell him the whole story, either. She already knew it was her fault that those men had accosted her. Nor did she want to upset her father when he looked so happy. He obviously felt that the bishop's news was about him. She wondered what an English bishop could say that would make him happy. He didn't even remember anything about England since he was an infant when he was exiled. And she knew he loved Hungary more than any other country. She'd have to be patient.

"You would do well to utilize the chapel more often. But tonight, we feast with Bishop Ealdred, Abbot Alwyn and the English embassy and you know the rule: no sad faces in the great hall. This is an exciting night."

"Yes, Father. Thank you. Do you already know what the exciting news is?"

"I choose not to speculate, lest I'm disappointed when I hear."

Relieved, she dared to look up. Her father was a handsome man, tall and lean. His beard had been freshly trimmed and the fringe of hair on his forehead was neatly shaped and combed.

They'd left his hair long and curly in the back, and she was consoled by the scent of rosemary that had been combed into it.

Edward's eyes softened to look at Margaret. He suspected tonight might be hard on her. Of his three children, this eldest one tugged hardest at his heart. She was as complex as a spider's web: delicate, yet tough, and a dedicated servant of the Lord Jesus.

King István, Hungary's first Christian king, would have approved of her piety. The man had been a lion. Edward wished he'd known him, but István died before Edward, Agatha and Edward's younger brother, Edmund, arrived in Hungary. The king had already converted the country to Christendom, and if he'd been brutal to his enemies, well, being brutal was sometimes necessary to show pagan subjects the way to God.

Edward knelt, putting himself at eye level with his daughter.

"We have distinguished guests tonight. Let's give them a welcome befitting their station. Smile, Margaret, all is forgiven."

"Yes, Father."

She'd beg for the Lord's mercy tomorrow and vowed that she'd do so inside the chapel.

"Children, tonight I will honor my father, King Edmund Ironside, by wearing his crown. It has been hidden in London since he died, but the bishop has brought it with him, for which I'm most grateful."

Margaret had never heard about this crown. Her father stood up, looking taller than ever and displaying an exceptionally confident bearing.

"Would that the kingdom of England lay encircled inside that crown for you, Edward," said Agatha.

Margaret was taken aback. Didn't her mother know that he couldn't possibly want to rule a country he knew nothing about? That would never make him happy. But she didn't dare say anything, especially after her horrible day.

"Perhaps my father prays for me tonight. Agatha, your ladies have a coronet ready for you - the ancient crown Yaroslav gave you in Kiev - you recall, yes? Etel, you will herd the children to the great hall. The sun has set, the banners are lining the walls, the musicians are playing, and I'm certain that the gossip is flying."

He turned to Margaret and said, "The chess board has been set up for tomorrow morning, when I will destroy your army. Do you accept my challenge?"

"Of course," said Margaret, "but if you destroy my army, it's only by God's mercy."

She grinned from ear to ear. All was well, again. Playing *sakk,* or chess, was the only time she had her father all to herself. Edward gave her a quick wink, inhaled sharply and left; his thoughts already having moved elsewhere.

CHAPTER THREE:

Edward's Feast

*T*HE evening air heaved with the intensity amid the excitement of the guests. Their gaily adorned horses pawed the ground, snorting the cold air through quivering nostrils, and jerking their heads with impatience. It was easy to distinguish which horses belonged to the Hungarians and which to the English. The Hungarians' obsession with magnificent horses ran in their blood, bequeathed to them by their Magyar forefathers. The Hungarian horses dwarfed the smaller mounts of the English. Luckily, the English groomsmen couldn't understand the graphic remarks the Hungarians made about the "girlish English mounts" and the correlation between the size of a horse's manhood and that of its owner.

On their part, the English were repulsed by the Hungarian habit of slitting their horses' nostrils and branding them heavily. It was barbaric, they thought, as were the Hungarians.

Meanwhile, Etel was simply in a hurry. She inspected the children with a practiced once-over, adjusting and straightening imperceptible flaws with expert fingers. When all looked correct to her, she herded them down the hallway: Margaret first, then Cristina, and finally Edgar, who zigzagged behind, slapping the damp walls as he went.

"All right, children, sit here. No, Edgar, I said, sit here," Etel said, picking him up and plopping him down on a bench in front of the two large wool tapestries that mitigated the cold drafts wafting down the castle's hallways.

The children waited with great anticipation, amusing themselves by watching the smoky torchlight dance on the walls and listening to the gaiety vibrating through the door. Its hum sounded to Margaret like a giant beehive. She wondered how the bishop's news could possibly live up to such anticipation. The children wiggled their feet in time to the music until Edgar got bored and began making rude noises. Margaret tapped his knee.

"That's enough, Edgar."

Nursemaid Etel openly favored the five-year-old. She'd admitted once that she'd pined for him when as an infant he'd been sent away to a wet nurse. For now, at least, he was still young enough to need her. The other two were ready to leave the castle for school.

"I'm Edgar's caretaker, Margaret. I'll chastise him. No need for you to interfere."

Margaret responded quietly.

"We mustn't spoil him, dear Etel. The road to the Lord is both a straight and a narrow way."

Etel snapped at Margaret.

"Of all days, Margaret, you've no right to criticize your brother."

Margaret flushed with embarrassment.

"Please forgive me."

She knew she must still be out of grace with the Lord. She couldn't do anything right.

They were interrupted by the sound of footsteps. Edward and Agatha appeared from around the corner, striding purposefully, followed by the *senechal*.

Margaret forgot about her transgressions.

"Mother!" she said, jumping to her feet. "You look beautiful!"

Cristina was too amazed to speak.

Agatha preened for her girls.

"They plucked my eyebrows, and then painted a most lovely color from our garden's belladonna berries on my cheeks and fingernails." She held out a hand for her girls to admire. "Look at my nails."

They were bright as the berries.

Margaret was mesmerized by her mother's magnificence. Agatha casually tossed her hair to one side so the girls could see how long the hair extensions made her already lengthy locks. Margaret could smell the rose water rinse as the hair flew by her face.

Agatha heard laughter coming through the door and it seemed to make her lose her composure for a moment. She fussed with her chemise. Margaret wondered why her mother would be nervous about tonight's festivities. She studied her bright green silk gown with its band of yellow at the hem and gold embroidery accentuating the neckline. The dress was sewn in a style Margaret had not seen before, with large, open sleeves that nearly brushed the floor when Agatha's arms were at her side, sleeves she'd made no attempt to keep closed with metal clasps. Encircling her head beneath her *couvrechef* was the ancient garnet-bejeweled coronet, gleaming in the torchlight. She wore no cloak tonight, instead revealing her shapely contours beneath snugger-than-normally worn fabric. A thin belt accented her waistline, and each of her delicate fingers was encircled with a gold ring. Edward wore gold jewelry as well, most notably his father's magnificent crown, but also a large gold ring on his right hand, its swirls studded with emeralds and amethyst. She'd never seen them so elegantly dressed.

Edgar was riveted by Edward's scabbard.

"Father, you're wearing your sword tonight. I want one, too. Please? Please?"

"No, Edgar. Not until you're ready and have earned it. It's time we greet our guests." He offered his arm to Agatha. "Shall we?"

The *seneschal* gave the door a mighty shove and clapped his hands, signaling the *olifant* player to commence blowing his elephant tusk. The crowd hushed to hear the grand introduction, "Prince Edward Edmundson, Edward the Exile of the House of Wessex welcomes you to his estate, "Réka vár, the Castle Réka." The drums and horns joined in a jubilant tune and the crowd cheered as Edward and Agatha strode into the hall and onto the raised platform, waving and smiling, their faces glowing golden in the dancing torches.

Next came the children. Etel placed her hands on Margaret's shoulders, shouting over the din.

"Lead your siblings onto the platform and stand next to your mother. Count to ten and then come back to me. Hold hands, children. Edgar, I said to please hold hands! Lord Goose, let's pretend you're a knight holding onto a dragon's tail … Lord Goose! Please just hold Cristina's hand for a …! Oh, heavens, Edgar, fine, close enough. Hold onto her chemise. Just … just go!"

The children clambered up the elevated platform, which gave them a splendid view of the entire hall. Margaret absorbed the magnificence stretching out before her. The great room was barely recognizable, magically transformed into a glorious forest with small, golden trees everywhere, replete with stuffed birds perched upon their branches. She could almost hear them chirping. Rushes strewn across the planked flooring became the leafy floor of a forest. The tables shimmered in the candle light. It was magnificent.

The animals populating the forest scene were the nobility, laughing and gossiping in their Paris silks and brocades, ermine-trimmed wool tunics, and soft leather belts. Accessorizing their outfits were looks of happy anticipation.

Even the thick walls of the great hall were brightly clad, studded with tapestries and banners. Nobles for miles around were in attendance, so many, not including the English retinue that had accompanied the bishop, that the great room was full. Margaret had never seen it so animated.

Jongleurs, itinerant performers who traveled with the minstrels as their assistants, cavorted through the crowd, walking on their hands, purposely bumping into guests and gesturing with their feet as though they were hands, mimicking conversation, stroking women's faces with their toes and tugging on men's cloaks, eliciting uproarious laughter and not a few lewd comments about the various uses for dexterous toes.

Across the room, minstrels, doubling as jugglers, entertained the guests by tossing knives.

Margaret took it all in, inhaling the thick scents of burning logs and heavily perfumed women. Loud pops sprang from the burning logs in the huge fireplace, shooting sparks up the chimney. She smiled. Some of the dresses in the room were as red as the shooting sparks.

Against the background of such splendidly colorful clothing, the black robes of the Benedictines stood out like fruit flies on strawberries. Margaret searched for Ludmila, hoping she'd been invited, but as a lay sister, she didn't have enough stature to warrant inclusion.

Caught up in the excitement, the children had overstayed their moment of glory on the platform and a stern Etel was flailing her arms, motioning them down.

Once at Etel's side, Margaret's excitement spilled over.

"The *jongleurs* are so funny, walking on their hands. And did you see the jugglers throwing real knives? They're magnificent - brave as warriors!"

Etel frowned.

"The jugglers are decent men, but those itinerant *jongleurs* are shifty. Don't speak to them. Those minstrels the bishop has brought with him look French, not English to me, sent by your great-uncle King Edward, I'm sure. Did you know that the Confessor lived in Normandy during his exile and when he returned to England, he brought back with him Abbot Robert of Jumièges and made him a bishop? And not just any bishop, but Bishop of London, for heaven's sake. Imagine, a Norman being Bishop of London. What a world, when one of the kings of England's closest confidant is French. Foolishness. The Normans are not to be trusted, I tell you."

Margaret responded with an absent head bob, for something was happening at the far end of the room: a rope was being strung between iron rungs on opposing walls, the full length of the hall, stretching high above everyone's heads. An acrobat in a tight, shiny costume flexed his muscles, garnering attention and bowing to Edward and Agatha before climbing a ladder. He bowed again at the top, eliciting hearty applause. Cautiously, carefully, he placed a foot on the rope, toe first. A nearby noblewoman, overcome with fear, screamed and fainted into the arms of her annoyed husband.

Margaret thought the danger was delicious. A tightrope walker reminded her of Jesus walking on the water in the Gospel of Matthew. She hoped the performer had more faith than the Apostle Peter did, since Jesus had to save him from drowning after Peter doubted the Lord's power. She wondered if Jesus would even bother to save a tightrope walker, since it a was frivolous, albeit, mesmerizing talent.

Her parents weren't paying attention; they were busy drinking the English red wine the bishop had brought as a gift from Edward the Confessor. Their gold goblets flashed in their hands as they laughed, sharing an intimate conversation. They were more interested in each other than in the entertainment.

But for the rest of the crowd, the very walls of the castle held their breath while the tightrope walker inched his way across the thick woven fiber, nearly losing his balance halfway across, before miraculously recovering it. Margaret frowned, suspecting that he'd feigned the misstep, but Cristina gasped and many of the noblewomen were clutching their prettily heaving bosoms.

The guests gave the performer thunderous approval when he reached the other side and climbed down, encouraging him to bow over and over. He strung out the applause by striking poses of bravado, wisely exiting just before the cheering died down.

The *seneschal* drummed his fingers on the table, waiting impatiently for the noblewomen to regain their composure before moving the evening along. He had only to nod, and the musicians and their thirty harps, ten viols and five bladder pipes sent sweets notes tumbling across the room, which in turn, cued a cluster of burly servants to carry in a large cauldron containing wine to fill at least three hundred cups. Hoisting it on the count of three, their grunts helped them swing the cauldron's large hooks onto a thick iron bar that was attached to a massive wooden beam.

Servants carrying trays bearing carved wooden cups lined up at the pot for the master wine steward to fill. He handed out the drinks to guests eager to begin an evening of liberal drinking.

Margaret and her siblings waited for their drinks to be brought to them.

Cristina squealed, "Look, Margaret. Here he comes!"

Indeed, a handsome young page with coal-black hair, soft cheeks and a dimpled chin approached, bearing a copper goblet in each hand. Cristina was smitten with the boy, and Margaret winced when he ignored her little sister, stopping directly in front of her to gaze into her blue eyes, smiling shyly. Margaret took her cup of *hipocras*, the sweet, spiced wine.

"Do you know my lovely sister, Cristina? I believe you two are the same age."

Cristina smiled and giggled.

"Nice to meet you," she said, her face as pink as spring blossoms.

The page gave Cristina her goblet, bowing and smiling to Margaret again before walking away. Margaret threw an arm around her little sister, knowing her sister's heart lay crumpled in her chest.

Cristina whimpered. "I'm certain he likes you, not me. It's always that way. You're the pretty one. My hair is too curly, and my legs are short."

"Oh, no, that's not true. You're beautiful. He's simply too shy to show his love for you," said Margaret. She couldn't bear to see Cristina in such pain. "He doesn't care a flea hop about me - that's why he looks me straight in the eye. Yes, I'm positive it's you he's pining for, which explains why he is afraid to look at you."

"Do you really think so?" Cristina lifted her chin.

"Yes, dear sister. Now, sip your wine - I can smell the sugar, cinnamon and that touch of spikenard for St. Joseph - and you'll soon realize I'm right. You'll understand these things when you're my age."

Actually, Margaret understood none of "these things," but she took her own advice and drank some wine: one sweet sip, two sweet sips, one big gulp and suddenly her joints loosened, her heart lightened, the fright she'd suffered in the forest was forgotten for now. Her feet tapped to the music.

"Will you dance tonight?" asked Cristina. "You hardly ever dance."

Margaret smiled. "Yes, why not? Let's dance *La Farandole!*"

The children held hands as Margaret led them, skipping and snaking their way between guests before forming a small circle to dance a *carole*. Edgar jumped about like a grasshopper, until Margaret finally burst out laughing at his unbridled clumsiness. Her laughter, as melodic as the birds of the forest, was a rare display of gaiety from the solemn girl, as surprising to her as it was to her siblings, but her mood was wine-inspired tonight. The drink made her forget about the awful day and blinded her to the lingering looks of men who observed her beauty, envying the man who'd take her virginity one day.

CHAPTER FOUR:

Distinguished Enemies

*T*HE girls were still doubled over in laughter at Edgar's gyrations when the *oliphant* player blew his carved ivory tusk again, hushing the room as fast as a squashed grasshopper. The far door swung open. Edward raised a cup of welcome in anticipation of Bishop Ealdred of Worcester's grand entrance.

The bishop was a fastidious man and the very air stilled when he walked in, as though it feared to muss his hair. He was followed by a subdued Abbot Alwyn of Ramsey - not subdued by nature, but because the bishop's exaggerated perfection left little room for anyone else to be noticed. Alywyn's cowlick alone disqualified him from being distinguished alongside Ealdred. Behind the two pranced a line of English nobles, their noses in the air to make it clear they viewed the Hungarians as barely Christian, and hardly more civilized than the Magyars of Hungary.

Bishop Ealdred, Abbot Alwyn and their top advisors joined Edward and Agatha on the platform, where goblets of the English wine awaited them.

"To Bishop Ealdred of Worcester, our distinguished guest!" roared Edward, raising his glass and spilling a drop or two of wine in his enthusiasm.

"To Bishop Ealdred of Worcester!" the guests echoed enthusiastically, spilling more than a few drops of their wine.

Ealdred rose to his feet and turned to Edward.

"To Edward of Wessex! The Exile is found at last!"

The bishop raised his glass, a move he likely had practiced a hundred times, to perfection, for he was much too meticulous a man to spill wine on his vestments. His wine barely moved in the glass as he toasted, a control inspired by his military discipline, no doubt.

"To Edward of Wessex!" the English guests echoed, minus the locals, who were totally perplexed by Bishop Ealdred's phrase, "The Exile is found at last." Why would the English embassy think that Edward the Exile, heir to their throne, had ever been lost? He'd arrived here in Násdad in 1046, eleven years ago, with a very pregnant Agatha, along with Edward's elder brother, Edmund, from Kiev. Confused whispers floated between the locals.

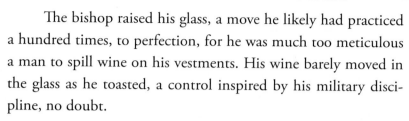

Happily, everyone's attention quickly turned to the troubadours who entered, walking in time to the music, half from one door and half from another, carrying their lutes and dressed as colorfully as peacocks. They bowed to the head table before taking their places.

Important stories were about to be unspooled in several languages, stories which the locals hoped would explain why Edward had seemed "lost" to parts of the world.

The bishop's minstrels began the tale in Anglo-Saxon. Margaret tried to follow their words, but it was confusing. She wasn't entirely convinced what version of Anglo-Saxon they were speaking; however, she picked out names and words: King István, Edward the Confessor and Cnut the Dane; and Sweden, Denmark, and Kiev.

It appeared that her father didn't understand the minstrels any better than she did. He stared intently at the fire, sipping his wine.

Cristina was completely lost.

"What are they saying?"

Margaret shushed her.

"Wait a bit. One of our minstrels will be telling the story in Hungarian. Then I think I'll be able to put the story together."

Before it was all over, parts of the Edward's life had been told in English, Hungarian, Danish and even a bit of Latin. Margaret was able to weave most of the threads into a cohesive story. She started to share with her siblings, but before she got very far, she was stopped by a gust of night air rushing through the hall.

The main door had been flung open. The *oliphant* player grabbed his instrument to announce whomever had arrived but had knocked it over in his haste, which could have precipitated a social disaster, had not the intruder announced himself in a stone-shaking voice, "I came us soon as I heard! Congratulations, my friend."

It was the boisterous Andrew, King of Hungary, come down from Esztergom. The shocked guests parted like a wave splitting in half, bowing as one to their tall, vigorous king. Ah, thought Margaret, he looked like Moses parting the Red Sea, her favorite reading at the Easter Vigil Mass. I must remember that, she told herself: if a godly and powerful king enters a room, people part like Moses parted the Red Sea.

Edward was elated by the king's presence. Normally, King Andrew visited only once a year. The two exchanged greetings in Danish, the language they'd shared as young men in Kiev.

"Come, my liege, King András, my friend Andrew, let me make room for you at the table."

The king leapt onto the platform. Servants scrambled to produce a goblet worthy of the king, but he waved them off. Along with the exquisitely carved bone handle knife on his belt hung his personal cup: a one-hundred-year-old Viking-crafted horn that held more wine than a goblet. He downed his libation in a few gulps, leaning over to Edward and whispering loudly enough for Bishop Ealdred to overhear, "Must be English wine. Hungarians would only use this for washing dishes."

The bishop silently bristled. He didn't like Andrew, personally, militarily, politically or as a king. Edward contained himself as host, but Andrew laughed uproariously. Despite his remark, he held out the horn to be refilled.

The *seneschal* unceremoniously reseated the bishop's lesser dignitaries at other tables. The men wore sour faces as they stepped down onto the main floor, trying to distance themselves from the Hungarian nobles in the throng with airs of superiority. The king was now seated between Agatha and Edward, pushing Bishop Ealdred from his place of honor to Edward's left elbow. He was not pleased; however, the bishop maintained his composure, lest he lose face as a man of the Church, but inside he was seething: he'd traveled many harrowing miles as leader of this embassy from England in order to bring historic orders from King Edward the Confessor to Edward the Exile, a man who'd spent forty years of his life killing time, and now at this moment of glory, Ealdred found himself overshadowed by a backwater king of a God-forsaken country that didn't even have any high-ranking envoys. If Hungary weren't a valuable buffer between Christian Europe and the Muslims to the east, the few who knew it existed wouldn't ever bother to visit it.

An additional matter caused the animosity between him and King Andrew: Ealdred, advisor to King Edward the Confessor, and possessor of a fierce, military mind, had opposed Andrew's bid for the throne in 1046, throwing his support instead to the reigning King Peter Orseolo in what he'd perceived as a nasty pagan uprising. Neither man had forgotten the other's opposition.

King Andrew knew precisely what Ealdred was thinking and he was enjoying the misery his presence inflicted. Andrew had fought for this throne and made no apologies for taking the holy position. Even the pagans had supported him over Peter, so obviously he'd been selected by God. King Andrew the Catholic was thoroughly Christian, a point his followers understood. Therefore, he was utterly confident about his claim to the throne of Hungary. Even cocky.

So, clapping the bishop on the back he said loudly, "Well, Ealdred, I haven't seen you in years. Let's see, our last communication was over that little uprising, was it not? Tell me, have you seen our King Peter lately? No, I think not. Actually, no one has. At least we know for certain that Peter hasn't seen anyone, don't we?"

The memory of watching King Peter's eyes gouged out as he writhed in agony, dying a few days later, was scorched in Ealdred's mind. Of course, a deposed king could expect to have his eyes gouged out, but Peter had begged like a child for Andrew to spare him, and Bishop Ealdred himself had argued mightily on Peter's behalf, yet Andrew had ignored him, a direct affront to the bishop's power, which was what truly bothered Ealdred. He didn't like being challenged. But the sound of Peter's screams still plagued his dreams. If the Lord was testing his humility and faith tonight, Ealdred was failing the test. The bishop downed another cup of wine.

Margaret, unschooled in the details of Andrew's ascension to the throne, reveled in the warm bond between her father and King Andrew. She knew her father and his older brother Edmund had met Andrew and his brothers at the court of Yaroslav the Wise, the Grand Duke of Kiev, an Eastern Orthodox Catholic, who'd taken in exiles hiding from their enemies. It was at his court that the young men formed a lasting friendship. She even knew that Duke Yaroslav had given his daughter, Anastasia, to Andrew in marriage. When Andrew decided to fight Peter for the throne of Hungary, Edward and Edmund had chosen to fight alongside him, helping him secure victory, for which Andrew was grateful. Still, Margaret was curious as a cat as to why King Andrew had congratulated her father. About what? Jesus was sorely testing her patience.

Edward wondered about it, too, but was overjoyed by the unexpected presence of King Andrew. Still, his heart raced to guess at the news he would hear tonight, especially since Andrew had made the 135-mile journey from Esztergom to Mecseknádasd. He obviously knew that the news was something important. But what was it, exactly? Could Edward's dream possibly be coming true, after all these years?

He tried to hide his mounting jubilation.

CHAPTER FIVE:

The Announcement

THE room buzzed after the minstrels completed their performance. Everyone had learned something about the prince's story, and it had been highly entertaining. The troubadours had spun the tale in poetry and prose – and in several languages, accompanied by strumming lutes and throbbing drums.

Margaret tried to simplify everything for eight-year-old Cristina and five-year-old Edgar.

She already knew much of the history because her father had shared how her grandfather, the great King Edmund Ironside, battled the Danish King Cnut for England until they decided to split the country in half, agreeing that whichever king outlived the other would inherit the entire kingdom.

"But then …" her voice rose in righteous fury as she related this part of the story, "… but then, one of Cnut's men arranged the murder of our grandfather on St. Andrew's Feast Day in the year of our Lord, 1016, so Cnut could have England all to himself."

"Really? How did Grandfather die?" Edgar was finally interested.

"Well, it's difficult to explain, but …"

The answer was so humiliating that Margaret groped for the words.

"They poisoned him?" Cristina prompted her.

"No … one of Cnut's men murdered him … while he was sitting in the *garderobe*."

Cristina's eyes got big. "You mean, he was in the middle of relieving himself …?"

Edgar made a prelude to a giggle but swallowed it when Margaret closed her eyes and vigorously shook her head in horror. The indignity of the assassination burned her soul.

"But Cnut wasn't happy about it, or at least, he acted as though he were upset. In fact, he had the man who did it killed and stuck his head high up on a post for everyone to see. Still, Cnut and his wife Emma, who was from Normandy, decided to harm Father and Uncle Edmund, even though they were only tiny babies. The king and queen wanted them at least maimed enough so that neither one could ever reign on England's throne; luckily, one of Cnut's own advisors informed a saintly Dane *jarl*, an earl named Walgar, about the plot. He convinced Cnut to send them to Denmark instead. But the evil Cnut sent a letter of death along with them, ordering that they be killed there."

"But why did he bother sending them away?" Cristina was fascinated. Even Edgar was listening. "He was the king. He could have done what he wanted to them."

"He wanted to look like a kind and caring king, and he believed that if the babies were killed in another country, the blood wouldn't be on his hands. But murder by proxy is a vile and cowardly act. Instead, Walgar and the babies, along with King Olaf of Norway and his son, went to Sweden."

Now Cristina was confused. "Sweden? Then what happened?"

"Cnut found out that they were still alive, years later. And his wife, Queen Emma was furious, because she was set on one of her sons following Cnut on the throne of England, but before they could get to Father and Edmund, Walgar saved them again."

Margaret realized with a shock that the boys were only twelve when they went to Kiev and that she'd be twelve in less than a year. How lonely the boys must have been. Home meant everything to her. That's why she was determined to live out her days at Pécsvárad Benedictine abbey.

Cristina interrupted her thoughts. "So, then father came to Castle Réka? With Uncle Edmund?"

"Not right away. They spent about ten years or so, living in Duke Yaroslav's Court, where they were taught how to fight, to love God, and to be great rulers. And they learned to speak some Nordic languages there because Yaroslav's wife, Ingegerd, was half-sister to our grandmother. Guess who else was there?"

Edgar volunteered.

"Mother!"

Margaret smiled. "Yes. She wasn't in hiding from anyone, but it is where they met. Father and Edmund became friends with King Andrew and his brothers, Levente and Béla, while in Kiev. They were in exile, because our King István had killed their father, Vasul, after gaining the throne."

"Why?" asked Edgar, puzzled."

"Don't you know anything?" asked Cristina.

"That's okay," said Margaret. "King Stephen made Hungary a Christian nation. But he learned that his cousin Vasul was only pretending to be a Christian and really wanted to overthrow him, so King István did what needed to be done. After Stephen died, his nephew, Peter, took the throne of Hungary, which put Andrew and his brothers, as the sons of Vasul, in grave danger. But the people of Hungary, even the pagans, rose up against King Peter, who loved foreigners more than his own people, so Father, along with his brother Edmund, fought alongside Andrew to help him win the crown."

"Where is Peter now?" asked Cristina.

"Oh, quite dead," answered Margaret. "It was the only way for Andrew to rule. And he was so grateful to Father and Edmund for their help that he gave them Castle Réka, and some forty villages, along with many honors."

"What about Mother?"

Edgar was a mommy's boy.

"They were married in Kiev and arrived in Mecseknádasd just in time for me to be born here."

"Why didn't Uncle Edmund get married and have children?"

"Well, I'm told he was and has a child somewhere, but he got the pox and died."

Cristina sighed. "I never knew Uncle Edmund."

"Even I don't remember much about him," said Margaret.

Edmund had died two years after arriving at Castle Réka, but it had only been tonight that she learned that he'd impregnated a noblewoman. He'd been forced to marry her, but his bad behavior in the eyes of the Church destroyed his chances to be king. And then he'd died.

Edmund's sin bruised Margaret's memory of him. She fretted about his fate on Judgment Day and vowed to pray for his soul at every Requiem Mass, because if he hadn't properly atoned for his sins, he was probably suffering in hell. She would pray that he at least be lifted up into purgatory, because her father insisted that he'd been a brave and kind man. She hoped the Lord would take that into account, because even though she'd been a toddler when he died, she remembered hearing her father sob as they buried his brother.

She ended her story there because the meal was being served. It looked like a display of gluttony to Margaret, but Bishop Ealdred blessed the feast, lest the guests feel guilty, by describing the excess as a prayer of praise for the Lord's generous "bounty."

The "bounty" continued to burst into the hall, each tray piled precariously high with meat: whole suckling pigs wrapped with string; venison that her father had hunted in the king's forest; five or six kinds of exotic fowl, including peacock. The huge head of a red deer sculpted from ground beef, including a real ten-point set of antlers, was served at the main table. Piles of soft white bread in large bowls followed close behind.

King Andrew sliced off a large hunk of the ground beef, stuck his fingers into the silver filigree salt bowl and sprinkled it on the meat until it was as white as a first snowfall. Set next to the salt bowl was a bovine horn filled with pepper, which he used just as liberally, the bits of black pepper sitting like bugs in the snow.

The less-prestigious guests were seated at the long tables placed between the gilded trees of the hall's "forest." They, too, ate with their hands from trenchers, hollowed out rectangles of stale bread, which tomorrow would be given to the poor: their "daily bread," flavored with bits of meat.

The main courses were followed by mounds of local cheese. Beer flowed and people ate and drank until they were as stuffed as blackbird pies. Groaning from overindulgence, the guests' attention finally swung to the main table, their faces rapt with expectation.

It was time to hear the news.

Bishop Ealdred was primed for this moment. He'd been selected personally by Edward the Confessor for this duty because of the impressive job he'd done as the king's envoy in Rome a few years earlier. Ealdred focused on executing his assignments in a manner that continually increased his status. Even his generous support of monasteries was calculated: it created an aura of holiness around him, something others may or may not have found authentic. But tonight, he would ensure that he'd be remembered as the man who personally secured Edward the Confessor's successor - one more rung up the ladder he was climbing. He couldn't be king, but he believed he could achieve a position of great power behind the throne.

Tonight, he would make this announcement the way he thought it should be made, the way he'd planned it, and in his own good time.

Ealdred was collecting his thoughts, mentally rehearsing each gesture and gauging the suspense he would create, when he sensed King Andrew lean forward in his chair, as though to stand. The bishop snapped to attention. He could not allow that devil, Andrew, to steal this moment from him and he leapt to his feet to preempt any such possibility.

Eschewing the protocol of his practiced formal preface, Bishop Ealdred of Worcester stood up and blurted out, "Oh, illustrious and rightful King Andrew of Hungary, we are blessed and honored to have you at the table for this great and historic moment, which I am about to share with all who have gathered with great and fitting anticipation. I will now read the words of the mighty and singular King Edward the Confessor of England, and so, my illustrious host," he nodded and bowed here to Edward the Exile, "and the good king of Hungary," he nodded and smiled at Andrew only to assert his victory at seizing the moment first, "I will read this most important document."

King Andrew leaned back in his chair, grinning, his goal accomplished. He'd only wanted to unnerve the bishop. This was a sweet night, well worth the mad dash from Esztergom down to the southern half of his country.

Ealdred was handed the parchment Margaret had seen being written in the tent. He relaxed as he broke the large wax seal. He now read it with great enunciation, slowly and ceremoniously.

"I, Ealdred, Bishop of Worcester, bring fond greetings to you, Edward the Exile, from your uncle, the pious and just Edward the Confessor - as devoted to Jesus as a priest, as chaste as a virgin, and a king who attends Mass each morning before going hawking."

Ealdred cringed. Was that what he'd instructed the scribe to write? It was true that King Edward was obsessed with falconry and deer hunting but putting it on a par with attending Mass sounded crass. He'd have the scribe rewrite the document before leaving it with Edward. Behind him, King Andrew muttered something derisive, but Ealdred ignored him and pressed on. "Our beloved and saintly King Edward wishes me to personally convey his sentiments to you."

He cleared his throat again to make sure he had everyone's attention.

He did. The horns blew and the drums beat as he solemnly unfurled the scroll further, to read the words of the Confessor:

"I, King Edward of England, give thanks that my half-nephew, Edward of Wessex, who still lives in exile, has for so many years been protected by the strong arm of our Lord. You will have heard this night how the murderous Cnut of Denmark swore death on Edward and his brother, Edmund. But our Lord Jesus Christ touched the hearts of foreigners, guiding them to save the royal babes. I hereby acknowledge that Edward and Edmund fought bravely in battle alongside King Andrew, and that Edward, who has lived an exemplary life in Hungary, and whose whereabouts we discovered only a few years ago - is due to the graciousness of our God."

Cheers sprang from the crowd. Bishop Ealdred continued, raising his voice even as he slowed his pace to increase the intensity and build to the rousing climax.

"Therefore, I, Edward, King of England, growing weaker with age, hereby summon Prince Edward Edmundson of the House of Wessex, and rightful blood heir to the throne of England

…" the bishop's voice boomed to a crescendo here … "to return to the country of his birth, in order to accept the crown and scepter of our great land upon my death, at which time I pray that the Lord will accept me, an unholy sinner, into heaven!"

There it was. Edward the Exile now formally became Edward Aetheling, now not only eligible, but summoned as future king of a country of which he had no memory, and whose language he couldn't speak, but over which he yearned to rule. At last, his patience, and his prayers to reign as a righteous king had been heard and answered by God.

Everyone clapped, except for Margaret, who shouted, "No!" but her protest was drowned out by the cheers of the guests. She was so devastated, she was afraid she'd faint and so sank to the floor, her head hanging between her knees, sobbing. God was still punishing her for praying by the stream and forgetting her duty, she was sure. Had she not been so upset, she'd have realized that the decision had been made before Ealdred left England, but her eleven-year-old brain only knew that once Bishop Ealdred had said the words, it meant they were leaving Castle Réka and she'd never be a nun at Pécsvárad Abbey.

From her vantage point on the floor, she looked up at nothing but joyous faces. What about her father? Surely, he knew her life had just been destroyed. She stood and studied his face. Even at this distance she could read the emotions flickering across it. They were swift and subtle, but she was graced with the gift of reading faces; so natural to her that she assumed everyone could see what she saw and was shocked when they couldn't. She observed each tiny movement of her father's facial muscles: first, a smile: joy and relief; next, eyes closing: humility and gratitude;

then a hard swallow: a vague uncertainty bordering on fear, and finally, the set jaw of a man prepared to don a weighty mantle of power. No, her father wasn't thinking about her broken heart right now. She knew she should be happy for him, but she wasn't.

Her mother's reaction was simpler. She'd been praying for this every day since she'd married Edward, and tears of joy streamed down her face. She was a pious woman, and so not surprisingly, she made the sign of the cross to bless herself: three fingers, forehead to chest, right shoulder to left shoulder, her fingers pressed together to indicate the trinity, her index finger straight, her middle finger curved and pressed against her thumb.

The guests bowed their heads and followed her lead.

"Praise be to God and peace to his people on earth," sonorously intoned Bishop Ealdred.

Not to be outdone, King Andrew chimed in.

"Glory be to the Father and the Son and to the Holy Ghost!"

Everyone blessed themselves again.

Ealdred had to have the last word. It was crucial to his ego.

"Lord Jesus have mercy on us, Virgin Mary pray for us and St. Michael protect us! Amen!"

Andrew couldn't top that.

The crowd blessed themselves a third time.

The evening's festivities now became devoted to celebrating with cheers and toasts; dancing and drinking. King Andrew raised his drinking horn time after time to Edward. There were no speeches, not even from Andrew, who by now had drunk too

much to give a speech – there was only music and jubilant plan-
ning; rejoicing and stories recounted, as hour after hour passed.
When people began to tire, monkeys dressed as jesters were
released into the hall to climb the hall's gilded trees and beg for
food from those who wanted the party to continue.

It was getting very late, and Etel gathered the children for
bed. She looked at Edgar, who showed no signs of slowing down,
and sighed. Cristina lay sound asleep on a bench. Both of them
were watched over by an ever-maternal Margaret.

Etel woke Edgar and took his hand. "Well, Lord Goose,
once your father is crowned king, you'll be the next in line. How
do you feel about being King of England someday?"

Edgar scrunched up his face.

"Would I get to wear a sword?"

"Yes."

"Could I tell people what to do and would I get to go
hunting every day?"

"Yes, almost every day. After attending Mass."

"Could I have someone killed in the *gardrobe*?"

"Dear Lord, I hope not, but yes, as king, you could."

"Then yes, I want to be the king. After Father."

A groggy Cristina looked at him doubtfully.

"Edgar, you need to grow up some, first."

"No matter," said Etel, "he has plenty of time."

Agatha blew her children a kiss as they passed by the platform. Edward was deep in conversation with King Andrew.
Margaret assumed that Bishop Ealdred had left, but as the chil-

dren reached the side door, he returned with a dozen or so English soldiers dressed in full chain mail, following him in formation. The bishop formally charged them to protect and defend Edward – to make the future king's safety their only concern until further orders.

Margaret felt a wall go up between her and her father. Her chest tightened. She could barely breathe. First the announcement that the family was going to England. Now the bishop had placed soldiers between her and her father. She feared she'd never have him to herself again.

By the time she crawled into bed, she was too distraught to fall asleep. She tried lying very still, hoping that if she convinced her body it was tired, sleep might come and calm her churning mind.

The castle had quieted down somewhat, the sound of horses' hooves mostly fading into the distance. Some guests would stay at the castle to party for several days, but others wanted to rest in preparation for the transitional process, which would begin first thing tomorrow.

Margaret saw a thin flicker of candlelight outside the bedroom door. Her mother was creeping into the room to check on them. Even though smoke from the great hall clung to Agatha's hair, her skin still smelled like roses.

Margaret kept her eyes tightly shut. Agatha laughed softly.

"You can't fool me, Margaret. You never sleep with your mouth closed."

Margaret scrunched her face guiltily and squinted an eye open. Her mother brushed back a lock of hair from her forehead.

"Are you alright, my firstborn?"

Margaret couldn't bear it. The words spilled out.

"Oh, Mother, things will never be the same, will they?"

"No, but they'll be the way they are supposed to be. This is the Lord's will. Your father is destined to be King. I am destined to be a queen, and you, my sweet one, are destined to marry a powerful ruler."

No! She didn't want to be married or to be a queen. She wanted to be a nun. Why didn't her mother know that? It's all she'd ever talked about. Margaret turned away. She didn't want her mother to see the tears. She just wanted her to leave.

"I understand, mother, I really do, so thank you, and now I'm finally sleepy. Good night."

As soon as Agatha closed the door, Margaret threw back the covers, putting on slippers to stand at the small window near her bed. She peered at the crescent moon through the window pane of nearly-transparent horn. Her beloved moon, Mother of the Night, always comforted her; for in Margaret's mind the orb of the night was an elegant, transcendent being, casting silvery peace into her heart. Tonight, though, the moon's waning light hung wearily in a corner of a dark chasm, looking forlorn and sad. Mother Moon was dreading, as Margaret was, the dawning of an uncertain tomorrow.

CHAPTER SIX:

More Than a Game

DESPITE countless prayers whispered into the ears of an unending night, sleep had abandoned Margaret. She thrashed beneath her blanket, restless, tired of being awake but unable to settle her mind. Finally, she slipped into a heavy cloak, put on a pair of leather shoes and tiptoed from the bedroom, stopping to coax a languishing torch in the hallway back to life so she could see her way toward the family chapel. She wondered if sleeplessness was just one more punishment from God and that she might never sleep again. If she begged the Lord for forgiveness, perhaps the Holy Ghost would at least grant her rest. And maybe the Lord would teach her to accept His will, because no matter what she'd prayed, they were leaving Castle Réka. Life at the abbey in Pécsvárad would continue uninterrupted without her. It made her so sad.

She paused at the entrance to the family's chapel, allowing its sweet fragrance to envelope her. Smoky incense had permanently soaked into the fibers of the embroidered altar cloth and clung with devotion to the chapel's wooden walls. She drank in the room's sanctity, pleading silently with the altar's ivory crucifix for peace.

She placed her torch into the back sconce, waiting for her eyes to adjust to the dimness.

She jumped. She wasn't alone.

A head and broad shoulders were outlined in shadow at the front of the chapel. She turned to run, but the shadow spoke first.

"Come sit, Margaret. I've been waiting for you."

It was her father.

Her heart still pounding from the shock, she knelt, blessed herself and sat in the chair beside him after brushing some fragrant herbs off onto the floor.

"How did you know I'd come?"

"Let's see ... you're leaving Hungary, and you still long to be a nun at Pécsvárad ... that would keep my Margaret awake, yes?"

She sniffled. At least her father understood. She knew she was being selfish, thinking only of her own desires.

"Father, our Lord has called you to lead the people of England. How can I question it, me, a miserable, little sinner?"

"Oh, I don't think there's enough of you to create a miserable sinner." He patted her hand. "Except, of course, for being disobedient by running off, even if it's to pray."

"I won't forget again, I promise."

"Obedience is important in the eyes of the Church."

"I'm sorry and I am praying for forgiveness."

"Good girl."

There was a pause. Edward spoke in a whisper.

"Have you noticed how loud silence is, after so much noise?"

"Yes, it echoes in your head. Is everyone done celebrating?"

"I just walked by the great hall. The monkeys have pissed and defecated everywhere. A number of people are asleep on the floor, trapped inside drunken dreams, which soon will be followed by ugly headaches. And when they awaken to find monkeys asleep between their legs, they are going to think they're seeing demons."

Margaret covered her mouth to keep from laughing out loud in the chapel.

"Father, I'd get in trouble for talking like that! Especially in the chapel."

"It's one of the advantages of being king - or almost a king."

It was time for Margaret to ask the burning question.

"Are you happy about becoming King of England?"

"Happy? Hm. Let me explain it in a 'Margaret' way: picture a stream flowing underground, far beneath the rocks and trees. No one can see it, but it's been there, hidden, for a long time. That stream is my longing to fulfill my divine destiny. The longing has flowed inside my soul, unseen, below the surface for forty years. Finally, it's above ground for all to see. Would you call that happiness?"

"It sounds more like satisfaction. And maybe relief?"

"Duty and devotion to God's will run deeper than human emotions. I'd say it's profound gratitude. I came to the chapel tonight to pray for guidance, and I've sent the other soldier to fetch the *archchaplain* for a private Communion Mass."

The other soldier? Margaret hadn't seen any soldier. Edward indicated the darkest corner of the chapel, where an English knight equipped with dagger and sword watched silently from the shadows.

Edward spoke quietly.

"A throne is not easily obtained, nor once obtained, easily kept, since kings are marked men."

"I'll pray for your safety every day, Father."

The door opened and the groggy *archchaplain* stumbled in, his hair as mussed as a prickly burr and his *chasuble* askew. He'd dragged a deacon to the chapel to assist him. Both had gone to bed after imbibing plentifully, thinking they had the night to sleep off their drunkenness. While the deacon fumbled with the engraved chalice for the wine and the gold paten for the bread, the *archchaplain* censed the altar, swinging the filigree silver *thurible* toward the altar to bless it with smoke - the holy scents of burning rosewood, cloves and myrrh.

Margaret watched the smoke curl upwards, rising to the ceiling, carrying their prayers all the way to heaven where the Lord God sat on his throne, looking down upon them, kindly, she hoped. She needed some mercy.

The priest hurtled through the Mass, desperate to go back to sleep, but Margaret didn't mind; she was going to be receiving Communion. Usually the laity only got to taste the sweet body and blood of Christ once a year, at Easter. When the priest appeared from behind the screen with the holy bread, she closed her eyes, letting His glorified body soften on her tongue. She even took a sip of the wine, holding both in her mouth as long as she could without swallowing. Then she and her father knelt on the floor to pray, lingering after the chaplain and deacon had stumbled back to their beds.

"When will we leave for Winchester?" Margaret asked.

She was in no hurry.

"We're going to London. Tomorrow the staff begins packing up the household. We'll need completely new wardrobes for England, clothing befitting of our new station and in styles similar to those of the Confessor's court, whatever those may be, which is why the bishop brought tailors with him. The *seneschal* will alert me when we're ready, but they mustn't take too long because I hope to celebrate Easter in Cologne, and we'll be stopping other places along the way."

"I'll work harder on learning English."

"You'll also begin learning French. King Edward has a number of Normans in his court."

"As long as I can continue learning Latin, please Father."

"Naturally. Are you sleepy enough to go to bed now?"

"No, are you?"

"Not at all, but I know how we can pass the time until we are."

They went down the hall, the two soldiers following close behind. At the door of Edward's private room, he turned. "You will stand guard outside my chambers," he ordered. "My daughter and I will have privacy. I'll call out if you're needed."

Margaret lit candles around the room to augment the snoring glow of the fire. Edward poked some life back into it.

Margaret's face brightened when she spotted the chess board, set up on the *tabula*: atop the board were large, carved, red chess pieces, patiently standing at attention, anticipating an upcoming battle.

"Oh, Father! Are we playing *sakkjatek*? Now?"

"Who knows when we'll have a better opportunity? Why wait until tomorrow? I hereby challenge you to wage war against me this very night."

"What if tonight of all nights, a little girl checkmates the next king of England?"

"She won't, but if she did, the next king of England would feel pride in his opponent's victory."

A ruckus broke out in the hallway: the metallic scrape of swords pulled from scabbards and shouts of "Halt!" came from the soldiers, who moments later, dragged Edward's flustered butler into the room by his arm pits, his feet trailing across the Spanish rug.

"Your Royal Highness, this man tried to force his way into the room without identifying himself. What shall we do with him?"

"To begin with, you will let go of my butler, whose ancient bowels you've probably just caused to empty, and from now on, you'll make a concerted effort to learn the members of the castle staff."

Poor Tamás, a lord who'd been devoted to Edward since his years in Kiev, leaned against the back of a chair, steadying his trembling legs and smoothing his strands of hair. He finally squeaked out a sentence.

"I noticed that you were awake. May I bring you some food and drink, Your Highness?"

"Excellent idea. Almond milk and a small bowl of honeyed pine nuts. No, a large bowl of the pine nut candy. Then you may go to bed. You've been through enough for one night, Tamás."

The soldiers stood at attention as the butler left, but even so, he flinched to pass them, careening down the hall with adrenaline-induced alacrity in his beeline toward the kitchen.

Edward tapped his fingertips together in contemplation. "Look at the chessboard, Margaret, and tell me what you see."

"I see my favorite *sakk* set, the one with the large and mighty king sitting on his beautifully carved throne."

Edward leaned forward.

"I'll tell you what I see: I see two worthy adversaries on the battlefield, waiting, trying to intuit the others' coming moves. They could choose to live without violence alongside one another instead of waging war, but here's reality: such a standoff is unstable, and instability is dangerous for a king and his country. To the glory of God, power often has to shift, and a victory won. I've lived in too many places and been in the midst of too much danger not to understand that. What I see is the history of the world in miniature: the hand of God leading His chosen side, the prayers that earn His favor, and the politics that achieve an honorable end to just wars."

Edward had lost sight of the fact that his audience was an eleven-year-old girl who, nonetheless, was listening attentively to him, wide awake. He continued.

"I also see Cyrus the Great bringing the Hebrews home from Babylon, giving them back their religion and land. I see Constantine and I see King Stephen bringing Christ to this country. A mighty kingdom requires a powerful crown, lest chaos encroaches on peace. Do you understand?"

He looked at the delicate face across from him.

"No, of course you don't understand," he admonished himself. "Why should you?"

The night had been long, the wine too plentiful and his life abruptly overturned. His thoughts were unleashed hounds, zigzagging wildly in his brain, trying to catch the scent of the many ideas he'd contemplated over forty years of exile. He wondered if any of them would work in the real world.

Margaret answered; her voice sweet with sincerity.

"Really, I understand most it, Father, especially about a strong king being important. I believe you're such a king, mighty and just. Our Lord will lead you to victory in war to protect us and when it's done, you'll bury the dead and lift up the poor. You'll be like King István."

"Yes, our King István unified Hungary and led the Magyars to Christianity. He was a mighty leader. But I want to be more like my mentor in Kiev, Yaroslav the Wise."

"Why?"

"Well, even though Yaroslav is of the Eastern Church, he still respects Rome, and he's a pious leader who has worked to change laws to make them more equitable. Most importantly to your mother, he's made it easier for women to own land."

"That's important to me, too."

He leaned back and looked at his daughter's face.

"You remind me of your mother. I hope you grow up to be as good a woman."

This would be a very good opportunity to influence Margaret, he thought.

There came a knock at the door.

"Enter."

What walked through the door was highly amusing. Obviously, the guards were trying to atone for their sins against the butler: one of them carried the bowl of candy, while the other meekly toted the pitcher of almond milk, leaving the butler only a tray and two lonely cups to carry. Edward and Margaret knew they'd break out laughing if they looked at one other, so both of them focused on the fire's flames.

The butler and soldiers looked expectantly at Margaret. Edward picked up the cue.

"Go, on, Margaret, try some. They brought it for you."

Margaret realized she was starving. She popped a piece of the candy in her mouth. The pine nuts were drenched in sugar and honey and then rolled in bread crumbs, a deliciously chewy treat. She poked at the pieces sticking to her teeth with her tongue.

"Delicious," she mumbled, her mouth working to chew the concoction.

"Good night, Sire," said Tamás, who bowed and left with his new friends.

Margaret nearly choked on her second handful of candy when her father produced a pair of dice from under a cushion.

"Look!"

He was triumphant about his surprise. Margaret was shocked.

"Father! We can't play *sakk* with dice. That's gambling. It's a sin!"

"Now Margaret, we're not betting on the game, and we're in no danger of missing Mass; plus, we've already been to Mass tonight. We're just speeding up the game, in case one of us …" and he pointed at her, "gets sleepy. It's deadly unwise to nap during battle."

"But if the chaplain sees us, we're each going to have to wash the feet of at least twelve poor men and probably feed them, too, as penance."

"I'm certain that the chaplain is asleep right now; and if we do get caught, I'll complete your penance as well as mine."

He handed her the dice, threw back some sweet almond milk and carefully selected two pieces of candy.

"I bestow on you the first move."

She rolled the wooden dice in her hand.

"Well, there's no use throwing for the first move since I've no choice but to move a foot soldier."

"Then choose which *gyalog* will brave the battle first."

She hesitated, her hand hovering over the board, trying to select which soldier to move.

Edward challenged her.

"How do you choose which piece to move first? Are you calculating how I might respond? Have you decided how many foot soldiers you're willing to sacrifice? And who will you sacrifice after them? It's the job of the horsemen to protect those of higher rank. And remember the element of chance created by the dice: roll a one and move a pawn, roll two and move a foot soldier or a horseman and so on. You can lose a turn down the road if you don't roll the number of a moveable piece. So keep your strategy loose enough to adjust …"

By now she was paralyzed, afraid to move at all.

"… but most of all, push away all fear of making a mistake. It's better to make a mistake and learn, than to ignore your options. You always have choices, in chess and in life. You can be happy or sad; helpful or destructive; wise or foolish.

"Forgive me, Father, but I don't think that's true."

Edward's eyebrows arched.

"Really? Tell me where I am wrong."

"Well, when a knife is held to your throat, you don't have any choices."

"My child, you may not have control, but you do have choices: you can fight back, you can call for help, you can panic or you can decide to stay calm, you can pray for the Lord to save your soul, or you can smile at the assailant and invite him to slit your throat."

"Those are choices?"

"Of course, and thinking through them keeps your mind clear. Now, I've left out one important choice. Can you tell me what it is?"

She thought hard. "I don't know."

"Take your time. The sun hasn't risen yet."

She sighed. Her mind was a blank.

"I just don't know."

"Keep thinking. I'll try to stay awake."

"I can't think."

"Yes, you can."

"I'm sorry, Father. I give up."

"Yes, that's your other choice: giving up, and it's the only unacceptable one. Make your move."

CHAPTER SEVEN:

A Queen's Place

ICE tumbled across the game board. Chess pieces marched forward or edged diagonally. Forlorn prisoners of war lined both sides of the table. This was a battle between father and daughter; a king-to-be and a bright little girl, each stubbornly ignoring the growing exhaustion circling overhead like a buzzard waiting for its prey to weaken. The bird would have to wait - the chessboard still crackled with energy. Margaret sat happily on the edge of her chair because time alone with her father was elusive. Carefully moving her chess pieces with her right hand, her left made unconscious circles from the candy bowl to her mouth.

"I believe your left arm has a will of its own. Are you actually hungry, Margaret?"

"No," she said, looking with surprise at her hand. "I guess eating helps me think."

Edward contemplated his next move. Margaret broke into his thoughts.

"Father," Margaret said, "why did it take so long for the crown to find you? It can't have been that hard. You've been right here for a long time."

Edward tugged on his beard. "Well, actually, the German king, Henry III did know where I was, and I'm told that Bishop

Ealdred was dispatched to his court two years ago, to ask for his help in finding me."

"Well, then?"

"It's politics, Margaret. When the Hungarians forced King Peter the Venetian ..."

"The Venetian?"

"Yes, his father was Italian, and his mother was King István's sister. So, when Peter was forced off the throne for the first time ..."

"There was more than one time?"

"Yes, Peter was an arrogant man, a ruthless man, more interested in foreigners than Hungarians. He was replaced by Samuel Alba, who lacked piety. During those times, the Hungarian people strayed from Christianity. They went back to their shamans and as pagans started doing things like sacrificing beautiful horses again ..."

"Oh, no!"

"They did. Meanwhile, Peter the Venetian took shelter in Henry III's court. Henry finally sent an army into Hungary that set Peter back on the throne."

"That's when you and our King Andrew decided to set things right, isn't it?"

"That's when Andrew decided to claim his right to the throne for the good of his country. Edmund and I wanted to help him, because we'd become close friends."

"Both Henry III and Bishop Ealdred had grudges against Andrew?"

"Exactly. Two years ago, Ealdred was sent to Henry's court to inquire about me. Henry distracted him in Germany for a year, having him study architecture and German liturgy and even gifting him with a precious prayer book before sending him home. True, Henry knew I was here, and promised Ealdred he would fetch me, but in reality, he had no intention of following through, and Ealdred wasn't disposed to deal with Andrew, so nothing came of it."

"None of that makes sense."

"Of course, it doesn't, not to someone who is pure in heart, like you, but kings and bishops choose to ignore people they don't want to help. The good news is that Henry III died, and that Edward the Confessor has finally recalled me from exile. That's life, Margaret. I'm not surprised."

What did surprise him was how well his daughter was playing chess. Her moves showed creativity, sound instincts and not a little aggression, albeit tempered by discretion. Now was the time for him to carry her to a higher level, while teaching a lesson in life.

"Margaret, stop for one moment, and look at the entire board. How many options can you find, and how might each one position you three moves from now? Think."

While she took in the board and remaining pieces, Edward continued to deliberate how he might turn this chess game into a lifelong moral compass for Margaret. Opportunities to influence her would evaporate once he was crowned and she left for schooling at a convent. He picked up his king, turning it over and over in his hand, considering his approach.

"Margaret, which is the most valuable piece on the board?"

"Well, the king, of course. The game ends when he's in the position to be captured. Checkmated."

"Correct. And which is the most powerful piece?"

"The king, again. He's by far the most important."

"I said the most powerful, not the most important."

"Oh. Powerful?" She was stumped. "Perhaps a bishop, since the Church is both important and powerful?"

Edward laughed.

"In France, they call that piece the 'fool.' No, this is the most powerful piece," he said, handing her his queen. Margaret's blue eyes widened; two large sapphires set in her heart-shaped face.

"The queen is the most powerful piece?"

"Some call her an advisor, or something similar, but I find 'queen' appropriate because she can move in any direction, she protects the king and more often than not, she's the one to checkmate an opponent. A queen is the most powerful person in a king's life. Your mother has been that for me since we married."

"Mother? I mean, I see her supervising the castle, but everyone considers you the powerful one, Father, not Mother."

"Precisely my point. It's a bit of deception. Like the chess piece, Margaret, your mother can move in any direction without attracting much notice. She observes the court moving around me, placing herself between me and those who would undermine me, while evaluating complicated situations with clarity. I always take her opinion into consideration before making any decision. I would fear the throne of England if not for Agatha."

Margaret was shocked. She stared at the queen in her hand.

"She doesn't show it."

"That's the crux of a queen's position. If Agatha let her influence show, she might not overhear threatening gossip. Your mother is a model of grace. But you mustn't tell others of her secret. She'd lose her power."

"Oh, Father, I'd throw myself into the old mine pit before I'd break a promise to you."

"I know."

She handed him back his queen.

"And I thought we were playing a game. Where did you learn to play chess?"

"While Edmund and I were living in Kiev, an Arab trader from Spain stayed at Yaroslav's court for several months. I even remember his name: ibn Hujayrah. We had a lot of time on our hands, so he taught me *sakk*. He'd learned it from a Persian, who referred to the king as the "shah," and utilized an elephant in place of our horseman."

"An elephant? On a battlefield?"

"Yes, amazingly."

The fire sputtered and spit, unnoticed by the tiring duo. But as the room slowly darkened, their lids got heavy and their conversation became disjointed. They were both asleep before the fire's embers collapsed into a mound of soft ashes.

Only a few hours later, the dark night had seeped like mud back into the earth, replaced by the morning's soft light floating down like manna. Birds sang and church bells rang, rousing the great hall's hungover guests who awoke feeling terrible. A noblewoman who opened her eyes to discover a monkey nestled between her breasts screamed and ran in circles, as did the equally terrified monkey.

Tamás knocked.

"Sire, are you still in there?"

Cracking open the door, he found a snoring Edward draped across the chair, one lanky leg thrown over its arm, his beard splayed across his chest. Across from him, Margaret sat upright, fast asleep, a horseman in her hand, her head drooping to the side and her mouth open.

Tamás collected their cups and bowl, glancing at the unfinished game. Edward was one move away from checkmating Margaret, yet he'd not made the move. Tamás discarded the notion that Edward would let Margaret win, because life didn't let people win, especially royalty. Unfounded confidence in her abilities would prove dangerous to Margaret. No, Edward simply hadn't wanted the game to end yet. Tamás shook him awake.

"Sire, Bishop Ealdred is asking to meet with you after Mass."

Edward wiped sleep's cobwebs from his eyes.

"Yes, of course, right after the *Missa*."

"Shall I wake Margaret?"

Edward hesitated.

"She's a special one, Tamás."

"Yes, we agree."

"Don't wake her. In fact, ensure that she is not disturbed, not for Mass, not for breakfast, not for her lessons. She is to wake up when she decides to wake up." He chuckled. "However, she's liable to be upset, because it turns out that playing *sakk* will make her miss Mass, after all."

He slid his queen one space. Margaret would discover she was in checkmate when she awoke. She would stare at the board, and reality would stare back at her. She'd lost again. It was a lesson she needed to face.

But her father had learned something, too.

"She'll beat me one of these days."

CHAPTER EIGHT:

Nyék's Humiliation

SOMEWHERE in-between the pseudo violence of chess and the bloody reality of war dwelt the verbal sniping between the Hungarians and the English. As Castle Réka prepared to move, a bickering, posturing version of war had erupted. No weapons were drawn, but insults were hurled, punches were thrown, dishes broken, noses bloodied, and a few ribs cracked, as civility slowly bled to death.

Agatha struggled to arbitrate the thorny issues, such as, who was in charge of the upcoming journey to England? Was it the Hungarian household, which the English called old fashioned, but the household considered family? Or were the English, Edward's link to the future, truly better prepared to lead the transition, even though they infuriated the Hungarians with their condescension?

Agatha migrated from room to room, following the sounds of disagreement.

"Yes, of course, dear Jakobne, you are in charge of making my travel wardrobe. Yes, of course, and Edward's, too. Well, what if we asked the English seamstresses to take care of the children's clothing?"

Jakob, Jakobne's husband, dug in his heels. Agatha may have appeared serene to them, but inside she wanted to excoriate them all, English and Hungarian. At length.

"Your insight is valuable, Jakob. I'm deeply grateful. We definitely do want to arrive in England representing Hungary at its finest. Even the children. Yes, I see your point."

She turned back to the agitated English tailors, explaining the situation in several fractured languages and using many gestures, and then addressed the Hungarian couple again.

"I've decided that you and your tailors will construct our family's travel and arrival wardrobe. The English will design our initial clothing for presentation at the Confessor's court, since they best understand the mixture of English and French styles that are popular there. Our good King Edward has not forgotten his years in exile in Normandy and therefore many of his courtiers are French. We will want to wear what they consider beautiful, too, *n'est pas?* Once you are familiar with the prevailing fashions of his court, we will naturally, rely on you again."

Agatha flinched at the sound of a wine barrel crashing against a wall in the cellar below them. Rising voices had crossed swords. Agatha ran towards the altercation. She had been expecting this, since the Hungarians found English wine decidedly inferior, and the English found the Hungarians themselves decidedly inferior. Their arguing was as pointless as it was relentless.

How would she get through these next few weeks of preparation? This transition shouldn't have involved her at all - nothing should have been her concern. There were servants and officials and exchequers and clerics to arrange the entire journey. It was this clash of cultures that required her attention, for the animosity showed no signs of diminishing. Agatha resigned herself to the idea that this would be a challenge every step of the way.

Edward had the easier time of it. In fact, his main focus was for his stable of Spanish horses. Fortunately, his *marshal* would be responsible for selecting Castle Réka's finest horses to make the trip. Edward would certainly take his favorites, riding each for only a day or two while carefully resting the others, so they would arrive exercised but fresh. On the other hand, the pack-horses pulling the carts would simply be switched out with local equines along the way as they wore out.

Edward intended to have the household on the road in two weeks. They'd stop if bad weather arose, and to that end, they would carry provisions and livestock to supplement the hospitality of castles, monasteries and hunting lodges along the way: those places obliged to provide for traveling royalty. Edward knew some of them were unaccustomed to hosting such large retinues and risked going hungry themselves come the next winter, without some help from his household.

Edward had dispatched the castle's exchequer on a final tour of his substantial land holdings, to collect outstanding debts and overall, to balance the accounts of the forty-plus villages under his control. Edward expected his return in a day or so.

As for the route to England, Bishop Ealdred's embassy had charted their route to Hungary on a map, showing pictures of castles and monasteries along the way. It was terribly imprecise, but the caravan could utilize local guides along the way to keep them on course. They'd require help, even if they knew the direction they wanted to go, since many of the ancient Roman roads were in such disrepair that they were impossible to follow. Experienced local guides would be worth their weight in gold.

In the meantime, the royal couple was trying to learn Anglo-Saxon, an annoying addition to their lives. The English embassy's finest tutor, Morris, had been assigned to them for lessons, but after a week of frustration, Edward put his foot down.

"I speak Slavic, Swedish, Danish and Hungarian," he told Agatha, "and I can read Latin. If my subjects don't speak one of those languages, they can bring their own interpreter or draw me a picture."

Agatha reassured him. "You'll pick up the language once you're there, anyway."

"I'm too old to learn another language."

"You? You're just getting started in your life's work. It's just that you're focused on so many things at once."

Agatha tried to keep up her lessons, but she was worn out from keeping the peace at Castle Réka. She was too fatigued to study her English lessons and her stomach was constantly upset, so that she could hardly eat. She begged off the lessons from Morris.

Thus, a bored Morris showed up at Margaret and Cristina's lessons one day. The Englishman was horrified by Nyék's instruction.

The English and the Hungarians were about to butt heads again.

"Please tell me what language these girls are speaking. It's certainly not Anglo-Saxon."

Nyék was outraged.

"Sir, I've studied English with three of Hungary's finest linguists."

"Try an Anglo-Saxon instructor next time, because your pronunciation is unintelligible. I can't even discern which language you're attempting to speak. What were the native tongues of your instructors?"

"Hungarian, of course. No, one was from Italy, Rome, itself. Such beautiful Italian he spoke. He also taught me to speak that language."

"I can't evaluate your Italian, but your English sounds like howling wolves. From now on, the children will learn from a native, and so will you. You'll be laughed out of King Edward's court if you speak this poorly. I will personally instruct you."

Nyék's face fell like an apple from the tree. Humiliated, he sat his bony bottom down on the bench, turned away from the children and examined his hands.

"All right, girls, let me hear you recite the alphabet."

"A, B, D, F, K, R ..."

Morris threw up his hands and glared at Nyék.

"Forget everything you've ever learned from your tutor, girls. We're starting over, beginning with the alphabet."

To Margaret's delight, learning Anglo-Saxon from Morris was joyful. She carefully replicated his pronunciation: his rounded vowels, crisp consonants and elegant cadences. She heard the language's melody and desired to sing it beautifully.

Nyék, however, moped his way through the lessons, drowning in defeat, his bravado wilted, his authority stripped from him. Margaret worked to console him.

"You're catching on so much more quickly than I, dear Nyék. May I practice my English with you during the afternoons? You'll certainly catch all my mistakes."

Nyék felt a tiny surge of usefulness ... and much guilt over the way he'd disparaged Margaret behind her back. He would make up for it.

"Of course. You know how facile I've always been with languages. I'm at your service, Margaret. I'll prepare you well for living in England."

She knew he was prideful, but knew his spirits needed lifting. She prayed that his sin of pride would be revealed to him in God's good time.

If only God's good time wasn't so difficult for Margaret. The upheaval at the castle was more chaos than she could handle. She desperately craved the quietude of their old life. She attended Mass daily, but with so many noisy strangers, even the chapel no longer provided refuge. She tried praying there later in the day, when most were busy packing for the trip, but then there was no escaping the angry echoes of friction between the English and the Hungarians. And those soldiers that constantly barreled up and down the hallways – they laughed incessantly and raucously.

Worst of all, she kept running into the unsavory character, Unwin, the soldier who had rudely touched her that fateful day by the stream. He gave her odd looks, such that she couldn't fathom his intentions; she only knew that he made her squirm uncomfortably.

She yearned for her stream, longed to enjoy the solitude beneath the rustling branches; to savor the chirping prayers of the birds and inhale the earthy scent of the damp banks. But she'd promised not to disappear like she had the day of Bishop Ealdred's arrival, so instead, she fled to the Pécsvárad convent, where the familiar sight of the nuns in their black habits gliding around the sweet-smelling herbal and flower garden in the center of the cloisters soothed her. Margaret took great comfort in the sisters' rhythmic day: a holy dance combining prayer and work, *Ora et Labora*, as Benedict of Nursia had outlined in his Rule, five hundred years earlier.

Her peace there was a two-edged sword. She could love it there with all her heart. It didn't matter. She'd be leaving it behind in a matter of days.

How would she say goodbye?

CHAPTER NINE:

The White Hart

ABBESS Anna Mária greeted her at the gate of the abbey with a hug, as always. Today, though, the nun saw Margaret's clouded face, and knew the girl needed someone to talk to.

"Margaret, you're being blown about by the winds of change, aren't you? There must be a terrible storm in your heart."

"I'm so sad, Mother."

"It's good that you're here today. You've arrived in time for *Sext*. The Divine light is at its fullest right now and we rejoice that Christ is being nailed to the cross. Join us in prayer and then we'll break bread together."

"I'd like that, Mother Anna Mária. Thank you."

The nun watched Margaret pray the noontime Divine Office with furious devotion.

"God, come to my assistance. Lord, make haste to save me ..."

A tear trickled down Margaret's cheek. Her tears were a torrent by the reading of Psalm 118.

"... I called on the Lord in distress ..."

Poor child, thought the Abbess.

"The Lord answered me and set me in a broad place ..."

Lord Jesus, she prayed, set this child in a broad place. She may act older than her years, but her emotions are those of a bewildered eleven-year-old.

"... The Lord is my strength and song; And He has become my salvation."

Margaret's shoulders were heaving.

Anna Mária regretted Bishop Ealdred's arrival at the castle and the message he'd brought from England. She'd hoped that Edward and his family would live out their lives in peaceful exile here, where they were safe and well-liked, and where Margaret was earmarked for the convent. The nuns had been happily waiting to include her in their journey of service to the Lord. Anna Mária yearned to help the girl handle the loss of her home and dreams. But how?

Ludmila had been working at the far end of the vegetable gardens when the bells rang for *Sext.* She'd run to wash the dirt off her hands at the *lavatorium* but was still late joining liturgy of the hours. As they ended, she hurried over to Margaret, wrapping her in a fierce bear hug.

"I won't let them take you," she cried, her sobs louder than Margaret's.

Mother Anna Mária stepped in. This display of emotion wasn't helpful. She admonished the lay sister.

"Are you questioning the justice of the Lord, Ludmila?" she said, more sternly than she felt. "We rejoice with the Holy Ghost's intervention into Margaret's life."

Ludmila hung her head. "Yes, Mother." But nothing stemmed her sorrow.

The abbess gestured, and a cluster of nuns formed around Margaret, leading her gently toward the refectory, encouraging her each step of the way.

"Margaret, how exciting England will be! And you'll meet your great-uncle, holy King Edward the Confessor!"

"Please come back to visit us soon; we'll be waiting for you!"

"Don't cry, dear princess, the Lord is pouring out His blessings on you!"

Emerging from the dark church into the fresh air and sunlight of the open cloisters felt good.

By the time Margaret was seated at the long table in the refectory with the nuns, her cheeks were dry, and she was smiling.

The nuns ate in silence. It wasn't required at this meal, at least not under The Rule of Benedict, but the nuns desired it. After a morning of prayer and work, they found it restful to quietly eat their greens and beets from the garden, two purple carrots each, plus half an apple, a bite of dark bread and a small piece of dried fish. Their austerity made Margaret ashamed of how much food she and her family consumed. She decided that from now on she would eat half of whatever was offered to her.

But what if that were insufficient penance in His eyes? Perhaps the Lord desired some greater sacrifice. After all, He was taking her away from her beloved convent, so maybe she'd failed Him. What sacrifice did He require from her?

The young nun seated next to Margaret reached uncomfortably for her wooden cup of water. Margaret realized that she must be wearing a sackcloth, a *cilice*, a piece of clothing made from black goats' hair, tied fur-side in against the waist, which constantly itched and rubbed the skin raw. Margaret had heard that one nun in the convent even wore the garment around her loins. Margaret couldn't imagine the discomfort, day after day, but she knew the prophet Elijah had worn a *cilice*. So had John the Baptist, using it as a form of cleansing himself from sin and as a penance. But while she recognized that the nuns were following an ancient Jewish practice, Margaret didn't want to wear one, ever!

Her hands trembled to realize that she wasn't strong enough be a nun. She didn't think that she could ever handle such penance, even if the devil tricked her into committing an unimaginable mortal sin that required an extreme sacrifice.

Her shoulders slumped. She'd already failed to resist temptation by desiring comfort over pain, and she hadn't even entered the novitiate.

The more she thought about it, the more agitated she felt, until vomit rose in her throat. She quickly swallowed it but remained horrified by her unworthiness. Worst of all, she was convinced the nuns could read the truth written on her face.

She stared at her food, her face turning the color of the cooked green cabbage laying untouched on her plate. As soon as the sisters began carrying their plates into the kitchen, Margaret fled from the refectory, refusing to look back, even though the Mother Abbess called after her with concern. She darted past the dormitory and its guest house, straight towards her little stream, not stopping until she reached her most sacred spot, a bend in the stream where a rock jutted out over the water and bubbles frothed beneath it. She plopped down on the rock, panting, too upset to kneel, blessing herself, hoping that the Holy Ghost would translate her groans in the heart of the Father, because she couldn't remember even one prayer right now. She had no words, only a wrenching desire for comfort.

She dropped a limp hand into the water, letting its cold froth play between her fingers. Touching a smooth pebble in the water, she leaned over the rock's edge to find a snowy white pebble, surely a pure, icy gift from God. Tears pricked her eyes. So, He still loved her in His infinite mercy, despite her failures. She'd bring this holy gift with her to England, to recall her secret place and this merciful moment.

She rubbed the wet pebble between her fingers, delighting in its sheen, when she heard someone, or something splash gently into the water. It sounded as though it were downstream a bit. Startled, she wondered who had discovered her refuge. She worried that the three soldiers had come back to torment her, and here she sat, all alone again. Defenseless.

The noise came closer. She smiled when she saw her intruder.

Thirty feet away stood a muscular red deer, four or five years old, she guessed, with a thick neck and impressive, ten-point antlers. Animal and human stared at one another, equally astonished to see the other. Margaret was intrigued, because this red deer wasn't red at all. She had never seen a hart this color, one whose fur was *albus*, whiter than angel wings, from his pink nose to his white tail. She wondered if it were true that such animals possessed magical powers. That's what she'd heard. She thought to ask the deer to grant her wish to be a worthy nun.

But the stag was trying to decide if she were friend or foe, rotating his ears, first both towards her and then turning one to the back. Margaret held her breath, staying very still. She didn't want to scare him away, above all.

The hart decided that she posed no threat and waded deeper into the stream, drinking thirstily. That this animal accepted her as a part of the forest made Margaret's heart soar. She saw his tail began to swish. She waited patiently. Sure enough, a minute later, more deer, stags and hinds, emerged from the trees to dip into the water. A more peaceful scene could be neither woven nor painted. Margaret sighed in contentment. She'd been given the comfort for which she yearned.

But, she wondered, how had this deer survived for years in the forest, as brightly as his white fur stood out? Perhaps the herd surrounded him, to camouflage him? She didn't know. He was obviously the dominant hart. Truly he was a magical creature, blessed and protected. Or, thought Margaret, as her heart pounded, was he an incarnation of the Holy Ghost? Was she looking at the Holy Ghost right this moment?

She devoured every moment of the scene: the sounds of the deer family lapping up water while wandering through the stream, the way the water flowed around their legs, the contrast of the hart's white fur next to the ruddy-brown coats of the others, the faint smell of the animals' pellet droppings as a breeze carried the scent upstream to her, and the love she felt being in their presence. She closed her eyes to plant the beauty firmly in the soil of her heart.

When she opened her eyes, the hart's head had shot up, his ears rotating wildly, trying to locate a sound imperceptible to Margaret. He began exhaling noisily. Margaret strained to locate the danger he heard. This was not the Holy Ghost. It was a deer.

There was the noise, in the distance - the sound of baying hounds. The *albus*, having located the direction from which the dogs were approaching, turned, snorting, and sprang away, leading his herd across the stream, toward the deepest part of the woods.

Margaret jumped up, screaming, "Run! Go! Go! Save them, Lord Jesus!" She wouldn't let the white stag be harmed. Surely he was the prize they were hunting. "Run, run!"

They disappeared into the woods.

"Jesus protect you," she called after them.

The words had barely left her mouth when the *ratch* hounds came hurtling through the trees, dead on track of their quarry. Margaret stood in the middle of the stream, wet up to her thighs, splashing water, waving her arms to distract the dogs from the hunt. Confused, some of the hounds ran into the stream and lost the scent, while one or two went through and up the other side, picking up the scent again, but hesitating, confused about whether they were supposed to continue the chase.

Bishop Ealdred and his hunting party reined in their horses as soon as they saw Margaret in the water, dripping wet and wearing a fierce face that dared them to run her over. The bishop already had his spear in hand, prepared to take down the hart as soon as the dogs had him at bay, which had been imminent only moments ago.

"Margaret," the bishop said, trying to be patient. "What's wrong?"

"Call off your dogs."

"Why?"

"Call off your *ratches*. Your hunt for the white hart is ended. The *albus* is protected. I know he's what you were after."

Of course, she was right. The bishop coveted that stag for a trophy.

"Protected on whose authority?"

Margaret felt she hadn't a choice. She lied, something she never did.

"On orders of my father, Edward Aetheling. The hart's white coat is a sign from heaven that he comes from both the forest and angelic realms and therefore shall not be harmed. My father says the animal has been assigned to the Archangel Michael, who will take him for his own on Judgment Day."

The girl was making it up. Ealdred knew it, she knew it, and most of his men knew it, except for the dull ones scratching their heads. Ealdred also realized that the next king of England would despise him forever if he killed the stag over his daughter's objections. The bishop dared not cross him.

Margaret had her hands on her hips.

"Call off the hounds," she repeated.

The hart was gone by now, anyway. The bishop turned the hunting party around. He'd get the animal another day.

Margaret stood in the water, elated by her victory, yet ashamed of her lie. She'd stopped a bishop, his entire hunting party and at least twenty *ratches* from killing a holy creature, with but a stone in her hand, and armed only with faith and courage.

She squeezed the white rock and smiled at the sky. She'd just slain Goliath.

CHAPTER TEN:

Opus Anglicanum

Opus Anglicanum. It was the bane of Margaret's existence. She was hopelessly bad at it. She'd always admired the silver and gold embroidery on all things religious, from altar bands to the numerous parts of priestly vestments, but she'd never imagined how difficult it was to do.

"Margaret, your stitches are uneven. You will begin again."

How many times had she heard that this week? English women were renowned for their flawless embroidery, and now, since the family was moving to England, it was decided that Margaret and Cristina should become proficient in the art form. They were miserable.

On the other hand, Edgar was ecstatic. He was being schooled in the martial arts. He even had his own small sword. Today his sisters wished they were boys and not girls.

The embroidery needles were dangerous, nonetheless. Tiny swords, that's what they were. Margaret had stabbed herself repeatedly with the weapons until her fingers bled onto the practice fabric, bringing chastisement upon her head yet again.

"Margaret, you must constantly check your hands and fingers as you stitch. Even a drop of blood renders the fabric unusable for a *Missa*. You cannot expect a priest to wear vestments with a woman's blood on it, for heaven's sake, unless you are the Virgin Mary."

"Don't worry," whispered her Cristina, "Edgar may get a sword to play with, but I envision arming troops of spiders with these things. Each spider could stand on two legs while wielding six needles at once. What do you think?"

"Who would you attack first?" Margaret whispered.

"Oh, any non-Christian country."

"An army of arachnids crawling up the walls of their castle would probably convert any pagans without a fight."

"Maybe. But my spider army would use thimbles as bucklers and hang their prisoners with nooses woven from spider webs. They'd be unstoppable."

"Not as unstoppable as your imagination."

Cristina dissolved into giggles over her own cleverness.

Margaret hunched studiously over her needlework, keeping a straight face to avoid trouble. Cristina, however, had already drawn attention from the nun in charge.

"Cristina, you will not giggle over this sacred work."

Cristina's laughter was replaced by frustration. She yanked the thread from its needle. Her lower lip trembled. "Sister, will a bear ever fit down the snake's hole, however much he tries?"

Margaret tried to deflect attention away from Cristina.

"Sister, I don't think the Lord gave either of us talent for this."

A young nun, the sweetest of their instructors, reached across the table to pat each girl's arm. Her earnest voice was calming.

"I remember how impossible mastering the underside couching stitching was," she said, "such fragile silk, metallic thread so difficult to work with, the unforgiving precision required to lock the stitches so they wouldn't unravel ... all of that. I cried nightly in my cell, begging Jesus to either take me or to show me His mercy. He granted me mercy by opening my eyes to the blessing in this work. He reminded me that although I will never get to consecrate the Eucharist, to break His body or to taste its sweetness daily, like the priests and deacons do, and even though at Mass I can barely see the back of the priest facing east behind the screen to consecrate the Host, I've been given great comfort, because, our Lord whispered into my heart, my handiwork, each gold and silver stitch, brings the beauty of the Holy Ghost to the Eucharist - and carries my soul behind the screen with it, there next to the bread and wine, in the decoration of the altar cloth and the priest's vestments. I'm certain our Lord sees our work and blesses us for it; sometimes I even think I see the shining faces of the saints behind the screen, nodding their approval."

Margaret and Cristina were captivated. The nun lowered her voice to a whisper and leaned in with a sheepish grin.

"Now, do I still wish I were standing next to the priest? Yes, I confess that I do, and that's my pride talking. I am a sinner. I remind myself at night that what we wish for so deeply often isn't what we really need, so I pray daily for the Lord to give me what He knows I need. And then suddenly, all the work I did the previous day becomes a joyful memory, because I realize that as I sew, I am praying with my fingers. That's why we don't get upset or give up here - because we're doing holy work and the Lord promises that such work shortens our time in purgatory!"

Cristina and Margaret looked at each other with saucer-sized eyes. In that case, perhaps the drudgery was worth the agony, because people said that purgatory was terrifying.

"Well," ventured Margaret, "that's a worthwhile way to look at it, sister. Perhaps you struggled at first, but now your work is beautiful. I'm sure it makes Lord Jesus very happy, since He's beautiful, and He wants us to make things '… on earth, as it is in heaven …' So, there can never be too much beauty in this world, can there? We'll try harder, sister."

"I just want out of purgatory as soon as possible!" said Cristina, rethreading her needle with enthusiasm.

There was an avalanche of riches being packed for the trip to England, and it was astonishing: piles of uncut precious stones, gold jewelry, crowns, large tapestries and thick rugs; carved wooden tables and chairs, trunks filled with embroidered leather shoes, silk from China, fabric from Paris, icons from Kiev, and wooden table settings for more than two hundred, including tall silver candelabras.

The religious articles alone required several trunks: from intricately carved ivory holy water buckets and elaborate priestly vestments to jewel-encrusted crucifixes and gold and silver reliquaries. Even though he had no country to rule as yet, Edward owned a kingly household, much of it gifted by King Andrew.

Living within the largesse of King Andrew's rewards, Edward's lofty status required frequent travel. Since he liked taking Agatha with him, many of their personal possessions remained constantly ready for the road, the difference being that this time, the entire castle household was traveling, bringing everything from the costliest peregrine falcon to the smallest wooden spoon.

The pounding of nails resounded across the valley as joiners furiously constructed extra trunks to transport the large household.

Agatha wanted to know Edward's plans.

"I assume you're eager to go directly to England?"

"I want depart as soon as possible, yes, and to travel a good distance before Lent, but I'm not going to rush to England. I think it's important I stop along the way to meet certain powers that be and to establish a relationship, especially with Cologne. The Holy Roman Empire is too powerful to ignore."

"I'll keep my ear to the ground along the way, Edward, in case a friend is really a foe behind closed doors. Where do we stop first?"

"Our first duty is to pay homage to King Andrew."

"Esztergom it is, then."

Getting there became urgent only a few days later.

"Agatha, please come!" Edward's voice broke as he flew past the children's door, his guards hurrying to keep up with him. Margaret knew something was very wrong. She stuck her head out the door to see her mother hurry around the corner.

"What is it?"

Agatha took the paper from his shaking hands.

The words caught in Edward's throat.

"Andrew is very ill!"

Agatha quickly read the message.

"Oh, no, apoplexy?"

"He can barely put words together and one side of his body won't move. He demanded to be hoisted onto his horse to ride, but he fell off."

"Oh, dear. Have they performed blood-letting?"

"Yes, yes, of course. He has excellent doctors."

"When will you leave, Edward?"

"Not me, but we, all of us: the family and our household, in no fewer than three days. The exchequer has sent a message that he is returning with some horses as tax payments, including several *destriers*, beautiful specimens. I'll give one to King Andrew and the others will travel to England with us, to prove to the Confessor's court that Hungarians truly do own the finest horses in the world. But first, I have to see András. Can we be ready in three days?"

"Well, the new wardrobes are not quite complete, but surely the tailors can finish their work at Esztergom."

"Good. Then two days from now."

That evening Edward convened a meeting of the Hungarian and English officials, explaining the urgency of the situation. The mood grew heavy under the flickering candles as the English and the Hungarians eyed one another with dislike. Edward chose to ignore the mounting tension. He had more important worries than this childish rancor.

"My family and our household will depart for King Andrew's castle in two days. Our monarch is ill. My plan is to remain in Esztergom until I'm confident of his recovery. Then we will continue toward England through the cities I've marked on the map."

Abbot Alwyn studied the faces in room, his eyes squinting in the candlelight, suspicion filling them.

"Where is the bishop? Why is Ealdred not present?"

Alwyn, paranoid by nature, assumed Edward had excluded the bishop for a political purpose; however, Edward had invited the bishop, knowing full well he would decline because of his dislike for King Andrew. The antipathy required political finesse at this meeting of these two cultures, and Edward was careful to utilize conciliatory tones.

"The good bishop informed me that he is continuing east, undertaking a pilgrimage to Jerusalem, which we pray, will bring him great blessings, but which renders him unavailable join us at Andrew's court. Knowing that he is taking some of the English embassy with him, I wanted to share the news with both households, to avoid misunderstanding. Bishop Ealdred will speak tonight to those whom he requires to accompany him, and they will depart with him at dawn tomorrow. Bishop Ealdred assures me that he's praying for King Andrew's recovery from the stroke." He handed Abbot Alwyn a sealed scroll. "Furthermore, he found it important to write this in his own hand. It's his request for you to travel with us to England in his stead."

Edward knew that Alwyn would be thrilled to be in charge, for once. Whenever Ealdred was around, the abbot faded into the background.

Edward was correct, for the abbot's face brightened as he read the scroll, and he suddenly appeared delighted that Ealdred wasn't at the meeting.

Edward continued.

"Those of you who are not accompanying Bishop Ealdred back to England are welcome to travel with us. In truth, we would be pleased for your company."

That was all that Edward wanted to say. He left the gathering in Alwyn's hands. He didn't care which of the English came along. He was preoccupied with Andrew's health. His worries went beyond their friendship - there was also the all-important matter of succession. If Andrew died, Béla, Andrew's brother, could claim the throne, but Edward knew that Andrew hoped his young son, Salomon, would succeed him. If the plans to secure an heir acceptable to Andrew needed to be hastily arranged, Edward planned on tipping any disputes in Andrew's favor. Hungary was his first real home, and he could show his gratitude by ensuring its stability.

After evening prayers, Edward sent for Nyék. The tutor nervously drummed his fingers on his thighs as he walked into the aetheling's chambers, terrified that he was being summoned to report how his English lessons were coming along. They weren't going well and Nyék was desperate to hide his failure.

"Your Royal Highness?"

"The servants are bringing in the library. I require your assistance in finding some information."

Nyék sighed audibly with relief.

The servants struggled their way into the room, carrying the massive library chest, taking care to set it down with a gentle thud. At twenty-eight volumes strong, Edward was proud of his library. He spoke crisply to the servants.

"Empty the chest, four volumes to a pile."

Nyék looked expectantly at Edward.

"Sire?"

"We're looking for the treatment of apoplexy. Isidore's and Galen's writings are in here, somewhere. Help me find them."

They thumbed through the pages with careful scrutiny, since each volume contained various, mostly unrelated manuscripts.

"What luck! Here is Isidore's encyclopedia, near the top," said Nyék.

"Good. I know he covers apoplexy. Set that aside. Now we search for Claudius Galenus, whom I consider the final authority."

"Ah, Galen the warrior!"

"No, he wasn't a warrior, but he understood them. He was a physician to the gladiators and also to Marcus Aurelius. Brilliant man. He knew the seat of the emotions and bodily functions lies in the brain, and I suspect that Andrew's brain is bleeding."

Nyék cleared his throat. He hesitated, then said, "Sire, don't you suppose that King Andrew's doctors are consulting their own medical books? I don't mean to offend."

He feared he'd said too much. His palms were sweating.

Edward grunted.

"A logical assumption, Nyék, but I won't rest until heaven and earth have been moved for him." He set down one volume and picked up the next, sighing and searching until he found Galen's writings in the last pile.

"Here he is! Nyék, I charge you to be responsible for keeping these two volumes with you, ready for quick reference. And be certain you're well-versed with Galen's medical treatments by the time we reach Esztergom."

Nyék's chest swelled with pride. "Yes, Your Highness! You've put the right man in charge." He cradled the volumes in his arms like babies. Bowing, he walked toward the door, relieved that his English lessons hadn't come up.

Edward looked up.

"Oh, and Nyék …"

"Yes, Sire?"

"How are those English lessons coming along?"

CHAPTER ELEVEN:

Confessions

MARGARET was a rag on the banks of her stream, limp, morose, staring into the water, too sad to move. Normally, the sounds of the stream soothed her, and the birds' chirping filled her soul with joy. And usually, she stayed still for so long that the flora and fauna forgot she was there and began to breathe and move naturally. To be accepted by the forest filled her with awe.

Not today. She was leaving Castle Réka, and Hungary, her only home. What would England be like? It didn't really matter - it wasn't Hungary. Cristina and Edgar were thrilled at the adventure, but Margaret was certain the pieces of her broken heart would never mend.

A flock of geese honked overhead. She rolled over on her back, idly watching them appear and disappear between the tree branches that pointed heavenward. Birds were comfortable living in different places during the year, she thought, flying long distances to breed and find warmth and food and then returning to their other home. But what was "home" to migratory birds? Were they capable of missing their "home?" No, she decided. She was probably alone in her misery.

She felt better to see a few straggling geese flying out of formation behind the rest. She smiled and waved at them. You and me, we're the misfits, she thought, flapping our way along with lagging spirits. We're as reluctant to arrive at our destination as we were to leave where we started.

Margaret pleaded aloud, "O merciful God, fill our hearts, we pray Thee, with the graces of Thy Holy Spirit ..." She'd heard the Benedictines use this prayer. She couldn't remember the rest, but today, those first words matched her despair. She repeated it louder. "O merciful God, fill our hearts, we pray Thee, with the graces of Thy Holy Spirit!"

It didn't help. She was still the goose trailing behind all the others, a reluctant misfit. She felt even less than a worm, because at least a worm would have accepted the Lord's will, and she couldn't seem to do that.

Staring at the sky, her eyes were drawn to something odd floating towards her. She sat up, watching the object, fascinated. A breeze stirred, wafting it away, then back towards her. Margaret leapt to her feet, holding out her hands. The object was a large white goose feather, loosed from one of the migrating birds, one of the stragglers, she hoped. It drifted gently into her outstretched hands. She'd held many a goose feather, but never had she been gifted one directly from the sky. She twirled it, guessing the distances it had flown, picturing the towns and rivers over which it had traveled and imagining the bitter winds that had tattered its beauty. She ran the feather's vane between her fingers, smoothing its barbs until it might have fallen from an angel's wing. She would carry this with her to England; this and the white pebble from the day she saved the *albus* hart. Mystical signs of comfort, they were treasures she wouldn't mention to her family, lest they call her pagan.

She cocked her head. Crunching noises were approaching from behind, purposeful movement accompanied by heavy breathing, and they were heading straight toward her. It was obviously a large animal, closing in on her location. Margaret frantically debated. A bear? A wolf? Should she run? No, the beast was too close, perhaps if she climbed high enough up a tree. She'd grabbed a low-lying branch when she heard a familiar voice.

"Margaret, are you there?"

It was a huffing and puffing Ludmila.

Margaret dropped to the ground like an apple.

"Over here, dear sister!"

Ludmila collapsed onto the nearest rock.

"You don't have to say anything; I can tell by your face. You thought a boar was coming to attack you, didn't you? No, a bear? Lucky you, it was just Ludmila. That's okay. I'll be thinner by the middle of winter when we're choking down slices of spelt and rye bread with porridge. Some months fasting becomes more pleasant than eating."

Margaret wrapped her arms around her friend.

"I'll pray for you always. How is it you always know where to find me?"

"I can't read a book, but I can read your mind. I think to myself, she's leaving her home for England, so where else can she be? I'm here to fetch you to the monastery. The sisters and brothers have a gift for you, but ..." she whispered conspiratorially, "... it's from our *scriptorium*, and not the men's, so I say, it's really from us."

"How kind! You know how sad I am, but I'm pushing that aside to go where Jesus wants me, even if I do cry when I think about it."

"We'll all cry together, sweet Margaret. Um, why are you cradling a goose feather? Have you run out of quills at the castle? We have many at the monastery if you need some. Or was the fowl that dropped it made of gold?"

Margaret wondered how much to share. If she couldn't trust Ludmila, whom could she trust?

"It's a miracle, Ludmila, and you're the only person I'm going to tell about it. This magical feather floated down from heaven, a gift from a flock of migrating geese. I think they were flying with the angels. The feather landed right in my hands. How is that possible without angels?"

Ludmila shook her head in wonder.

"I had a pear fall off a tree and hit me on the head once, but for you, the Lord rains feathers from the sky that land directly in your hands. You're drenched in grace, Margaret. This is a sign for sure, probably from one of the archangels, since the feather came right to you. I'm guessing it's from Gabriel, telling you that you live 'under the shadow of the Lord's wings,' or feathers, in this case. Your life is so full of the unexpected, Margaret. I think earthly destiny has no hold on you, only the divine."

"Perhaps that's it. I hope so. I knew you'd have an answer."

"I always have an answer. I've even had to do penance for having so many answers."

The two held hands, chatting and laughing as they walked to the monastery. Margaret made the decision to share all of her secrets now, before she left Hungary, because only Ludmila would understand them.

"And guess what, I was praying by the stream about a week ago, when all of a sudden, not far from me appeared a pure white stag, with pink eyes and a pink nose and magnificent antlers, drinking from the stream as though it were holy water. He had to be a spirit, I think, heaven sent, consecrating the waters of my little stream by drinking from it. But then the bishop and his hunting party came charging through the forest, intent on killing him."

"Oh, no! What did you do?"

"I stood in the stream while the deer ran away, and then I found the courage to command that the hunters stop the chase. And they did! I was shocked that it worked, but I didn't let them know. It was glorious, except for one thing: I lied to them. I told them that Father had forbidden anyone to kill the white stag. Now I'm going to have to confess my lie. Will you arrange a priest for my confession while I'm at the monastery?"

"Of course."

"When I got home, I asked Father to declare that the white deer should not be harmed, ever, and he gave the order, so it's not a lie anymore. But it wasn't true when I told Bishop Ealdred, so I still need to confess."

"You lied to the bishop?"

"Yes."

"What happened after the hunting party left?"

"I realized I was still holding a white stone in my hand, one that I'd just taken from the stream."

"A white stag, a white stone and now a white feather? Life falls gently on you with mysterious grace, Margaret."

Two of the abbey's nuns were looking out for Margaret and Ludmila to arrive. The sisters spotted them as they meandered through the apple orchard. They hurried to alert the other nuns.

Walking through the orchard, Ludmila glanced at Margaret with guilt all over her face.

"Since you've shared your secrets with me, I'll share one with you."

She pointed to the *cellarium*.

"You've probably noticed that the nuns are more, well, slender than I am. I have to confess that I sneak into the *cellarium* when the *cellarer* isn't there and take leftover food from the pantry – but only the food that's old or to be fed to the animals, I swear to our God, Margaret. I would never take food from the nuns' mouths. I just get so hungry, and they hardly eat anything!"

"I understand, Ludmila. I tried eating as little as they do for a while at the castle, but the food smelled so good that my stomach started grumbling and I ate it without thinking. You're not sinning, too much, except for the stealing part. Make sure you confess that."

"I wish I could control my hunger, Margaret. Why is it so easy to sin and so embarrassing to confess it? The hardest thing is when I have to confess the same things over and over again."

"Even the saints were sinners, Ludmila. You're too hard on yourself. Our bodies are riddled with possibilities for sin. The devil has no kingdom to live in since he fell from heaven, so all he can do is tempt us, hoping we sin, because keeping us from heaven is the only power he has, if we let him have it. At least, that's what I think."

"No one has ever said it to me like that before. How did you figure it out?"

"Things pop into my head when I'm alone and quiet. That's why I go to the stream."

The nuns could barely contain their excitement as the girls approached.

They hurried into place, eagerly anticipating the surprise.

Indeed, Margaret cocked her head quizzically when she saw them lined up in rows, standing silently under the arches of the cloisters. As a lay sister, Ludmila melted to the back row, lost to Margaret's sight.

Abbess Anna Mária stepped forward. A tall woman, even her heavy habit couldn't hide her elegance. She offered Margaret her hand, gesturing with long, slim fingers.

"Come, my dear."

She led Margaret into the cloisters' center garden, where the air was heady with fragrances: spicy fennel and lemon balm, mint, sage, basil and pungent rosemary. It was also the place where the surrounding nuns were best able see her. Margaret caught a glimpse of Ludmila on tiptoe, peering over their heads.

"My dear child," the abbess began, "we have long prayed you would join us as at the abbey, but we see now that the Lord has other plans for you, so we wish to give you a piece of us to take with you."

She glanced nodded toward one corner of the cloisters. The nuns there stepped aside to reveal three sisters flanking a slanted writing table they left outdoors in the cloisters for maximum light, weather permitting. One of the three nuns held up two quills, another a sharp stylus and a straight edge, while the third scribe cradled a bottle of oak gall and soot ink. All three had broad smiles stretching across their faces.

"Margaret, each of these sisters has willingly labored over a gift that exemplifies our love for you. They've copied holy text and created ornamentation on our finest parchment. Since all of us labor only for the Lord, they take nothing as a personal achievement, but instead, give all glory to God. No one woman is responsible for this gift which we hope you'll always treasure, because truly, it is from the entire abbey."

Margaret looked at these women with their pale, thin faces, their virginal bodies hidden inside night-colored habits, all smiling at her, enveloping her with love. She only wished she had proven worthy to stand among them. She'd have cried, but wouldn't, not in front of these strong and courageous women. They endured more stringent and harsh lives than she ever would.

Anna Mária stepped aside, for the monastery's abbot had suddenly appeared as from thin air. Abbot Máté was short, but every bit a Benedictine. He was accompanied by the *armarius,* the brother in charge of the monastery's *scriptorium.* The latter held a book up in front of the abbot, who made the sign of the cross to bless it. Margaret craned her neck, trying to catch a glimpse her new treasure, but he'd tucked it beneath his *scapula,* the sleeveless garment worn over his black tunic.

"Margaret of Wessex," Abbot Máté began solemnly, "we who have known the yearning of your heart to join us here in a life consecrated to the Lord, subdue our will to the Lord's. Your journey to England is part of His plan for you, and it's not for us to object to, lest we sin as Satan did – by challenging God's divine wisdom. Such selfishness is not allowed here. We fear being cast into hell with the fallen angels. But, since you have given your heart to us, we give this Gospel-book to you."

He laid the book into her outstretched hands and gave counsel.

"Inscribed on these thirty-eight leaves are the most important portions of the four gospels: the words of Matthew, Mark, Luke and John, as they relate to Christ's work and his Passion. If you carve these stories onto your heart, you will be a woman of God and a model for those who seek your guidance."

Margaret felt gratitude well up from her heart. The emotion was overwhelming, but she held back her tears because the book's gold treasure binding, added to protect the parchment inside, was pristine and she refused to mar it, even with grateful tears.

Instead, she cradled the treasure in her hands for a few moments before handing it back to Abbot Máté.

"I can't accept this."

A horrified gasp from the nuns sucked the air from the cloisters.

The abbot's eyebrows arched until they nearly reached his receding hairline.

"Excuse me?"

"I cannot accept this gift without first making a confession. I'm unclean."

Máté stared at the curious child standing before him.

"Then let's go inside and I'll take your confession."

"No, thank you, father. I must make a public confession, as the Christians did a thousand years ago."

The bishop was flummoxed.

"Well, uh, it's unorthodox, um, but of course, Margaret … then, well, go ahead."

She turned to look at each nun, for she believed her sin was against each one of them.

"Forgive me, Father, for I have sinned, for which I am heartily sorry. I confess to Almighty God that I have sinned through my own fault. I confess I am too weak to endure the harsh life of a religious, and I am ashamed of my love of comfort. Dear sisters, when last I ate with you, I realized that I am not strong enough to bear the suffering you carry. I do not love the Lord enough to give up my comforts, nor have I accepted the Lord's will to go to England. I don't want to leave Castle Réka and Hungary. Oh, and I also confess that I don't always love Nanny Etel because I don't think she likes me very much. And I confess that I lied to Bishop Ealdred in the forest when I told him that the white stag was under the protection of my father and could not be harmed or hunted. It wasn't, at the time."

The nuns were shocked, but not at Margaret's sin. Rather, they were excited to hear about the white stag.

One blurted out, "Dear Lord, you've actually seen it?"

"I thought the *albus* deer was just an ancient forest legend!" exclaimed another.

"As did I, but perhaps Hunor and Magor's hunt for the White Stag lives on?"

"Can it be? Is that animal immortal?"

"The white hart is part of a legend about our forefathers, the Magyars," whispered Abbess Anna Mária. "But also, I'd like to think it's a true miracle."

Margaret hadn't heard of the legend, but her reply was solemn.

"I looked the hart in the eye, and he looked back at me. He was magnificent, and so, when the hunting party came riding after him, I couldn't let them, especially the bishop, slaughter such a creature; however, what I told him was a lie." She paused. "But it's not a lie any more. I asked, and my father has laid a veil of protection over the deer. So now, at least, what I said is true."

She turned back to the abbot with an expectant look, awaiting her penance.

He had to think. This was a confession he wouldn't soon forget. He clasped his hands behind his back.

"First, for your reluctance to accept suffering and for questioning the Lord's will, you will say ten *Pater Nosters* and fifty Hail Marys, genuflecting in between each prayer."

"Yes, Abbot Máté."

"And for lying ... to the bishop ... do you mean you lied to the Bishop Ealdred? Oh, Margaret." He shook his head. "Lying to Ealdred!"

"Please tell Jesus I'm terribly sorry."

"How old are you now, Margaret?"

"I'm eleven years old."

"What to do with you, what to do ..."

He thought he'd already heard everything. Now he truly had.

She hung her head.

"You will perform two penances: the first penance for questioning the Lord's will. Then, for lying, you will wash the feet of a poor person. And because you lied to a bishop, especially the powerful Bishop Ealdred," he shook his head again, "as you wash the poor person's feet you'll repeat over and over again, 'Forgive me Jesus, for I have committed the sin of lying to a bishop.'"

"Thank you, Father."

"I absolve you of your sins. You are forgiven. May the Lord bring you to everlasting life."

He made the sign of the cross over her.

The nuns repeated the blessing, their fingers brushing against their habits making a whispering rustle, like pages of parchment being turned.

"Amen," they said.

The abbot sighed. He held out the gift again.

"Now may I give you the Gospel-book?"

"Oh, yes, please, Abbot Máté!"

He cleared his throat, mentally finding his place in the presentation he'd planned.

"As I was about to say, in recognition of your royal blood from the English House of Wessex, the scribe has used the style of lettering from the time of Charlemagne, in black ink, instead of our usual brown."

Margaret gently opened the brass clasps of the thin volume with wonder to see the rounded, openly-spaced letters written in sooty ink. Veils of fine silk lay over each gold-embellished portrait of the gospel writers: Matthew, Mark, Luke and John, to protect the gold from rubbing off onto the facing page of vellum.

"It's exquisite. Thank you, every single one of you."

"Study and embrace the stories inside with your heart," said the abbot. "They will guide you through life as you enter into the mystery of our Lord's death and resurrection. I will be accompanying your household as far as Esztergom. Should you need my counsel, I'll be available. Go now into the sanctuary to perform the prayerful part of your penance."

CHAPTER TWELVE:

Agatha's Secret

DAWN broke like a cracked egg, thought Margaret. It had a yellowish horizon rimmed with runny white clouds. She hurried alongside Bishop Ealdred's procession, hoping to be out of sight before he appeared. The line of nobles was the retinue that would travel with him. The English horses jerked their heads while the men in his traveling party were mounting up, as their women were assisted into canopied wagons and elegant litters. The bishop's cadre of soldiers awaited his last-minute arrival.

"Margaret!"

The voice stopped her in her tracks. It was Bishop Ealdred, emerging from the castle. She was nervous about seeing him. She'd avoided him since she'd ruined his opportunity to kill the white hart. She wondered if he were still angry with her.

"You're off to your secret place, aren't you?"

Margaret hung her head.

"No matter, child. I leave today. This is my last visit to your country. If you do see the white stag, remind him he's lucky his hide isn't packed inside one of my trunks."

Margaret was appalled by his casual attitude, but she knew she was culpable, too.

"I lied to you about the stag that day."

"Obviously."

"I'm sorry and I've performed penance for lying, but he is an animal sent from heaven, with powers from the angels. He has to be protected."

"Are you a pagan, child? He is a rarity, but he's not magical. There's no such thing as magic, unless you're a peasant and believe in anything. Even your little praying stream isn't special, girl. There are streams in England, too, and you'll discover they're all the same."

"They won't be to me."

He scoffed. He couldn't wait to leave Hungary.

"Are you arguing with me?"

"No, Your Excellency."

"Then I'll say it again. You'll pray by many streams, and face many changes in your life, Margaret, some desired and others feared. That's why your focus on the Lord is more important than having secret places."

"Yes, Bishop Ealdred. As He wills, always."

"Yes, well, His will won't always be obvious. Sometimes you have to bide your time or move in the direction you think He wants, until you discern it."

"Yes, Bishop Ealdred."

"Go on, Margaret. I don't care. Run to the place where you see His smile in the water. I envy your childish imagination."

She curtsied and sprinted toward the rolling hills. He didn't seem like a loving shepherd and she wanted to get away from him before he confused her further.

Edward and Agatha walked out of the castle to bid the bishop farewell. Agatha shook her head and sighed, to see Margaret running off once again.

"Agatha, let her go," said Edward.

"She should be praying in the chapel. We build places with beautiful statues for people to kneel in front of, so they don't have to pray among the earthworms."

"There are times to let a child be."

"You weren't raised in the court of Henry II."

"No, thank God. But I was raised on the run, all across Europe."

Agatha touched his arm.

"Of course, Edward. I know how difficult your childhood was, growing up like a hunted rabbit. Mine was nothing compared to that."

"But I am who I am because of Walgar and Yaroslav, and I thank Jesus for them."

Bishop Ealdred stood near them, waiting to say goodbye. He cleared his throat to truncate their conversation. Impatience was his overriding emotion. He'd completed his mission. He'd produced Edward the Exile and provided soldiers to protect him. The *aetheling* would safely travel to England. Now he desired to continue on to Jerusalem. He would be the first English bishop to make a pilgrimage there, and he bore a very special gift for the sepulcher.

This journey would accrue recognition and blessings for him, both spiritual and political. He longed for the pope to bestow a bishop's *palium* on him, a small, circular woolen cloak that would set him inside an exclusive circle of spiritual leaders, a symbol of the fullness of rank he craved as a bishop. He'd already accrued land, wealth and power in England. Now he wanted recognition from Rome.

He bowed slightly to the Exile to say goodbye.

"You understand the importance of this pilgrimage I'm bidden to make, or I would accompany you to your new country."

Edward flashed a diplomatic smile.

"I understand your situation, Bishop Ealdred. But if the Lord prompts you to, I would encourage you to visit our ailing king, who needs your blessing. But go with God."

Ealdred blessed them instead of responding, drawing a looping sign of the cross in the air.

"May the Lord bless you and hold you in the palm of His hand, bringing you safely to England to rule with wisdom."

He turned and mounted his chestnut *palfrey*. The horse snorted and shook his head in the cold morning air, tossing the silken tassels attached to his bridle. The bishop smiled with satisfaction. He liked everything in his life to reflect magnificence.

Edward waved, unconvinced that the bishop's blessing was heartfelt, but he accepted it at face value and hoped for the best. He watched until the English embassy and their inferior horses melted into the distance.

"Tomorrow it's our turn," said Agatha. "Do you suppose our eldest daughter will be back by then?

"I daresay she will, because we leave in the morning, with or without her and she knows it. We must get to Andrew."

"More importantly, we must get to England."

"And so, we shall, in good time," he said, waving once last time at the departing embassy.

He turned to his wife to say something more but stopped. Her face had turned green.

She grabbed Edward's arm as her knees buckled beneath her.

"I don't feel well."

He caught her before she hit the ground, but she was already vomiting.

"To the abbey for Brother János," Edward ordered a nearby servant. "We need the doctor."

He carried Agatha into the castle.

Her ladies-in-waiting rushed to Agatha's chambers, undressing her and putting her to bed. They lit rosemary to cleanse the air in her bedchamber and gave her herbal water to sip, clucking around her while she protested.

"I'm fine. Please. You know how sensitive my stomach is. I'll be well by tomorrow morning."

Edward sat next to her, holding her hand.

"We'll postpone the departure by one or two days."

"Don't be silly. It must have been something I ate. And a waning moon is never kind to me, as you know. I'm already feeling better. Go, Edward. You've much to do before we leave tomorrow."

The sound of approaching horse's hooves was faintly audible in the distance. The doctor was on his way.

Edward went to meet him in front of the castle.

Minutes later, János, the monastery's physician, walked into her chamber, followed by two other monks and a nun, all of whom knew their patient well. At the moment she was as agitated as she was nauseated. The doctor began to assess the situation.

"Lay back, dear Agatha, and let me have a look at you. You're very pale," said János.

"You're as observant as my five-year-old." She was too ill for patience.

He felt her pulse.

"Your heart is racing. You're upset."

"Of course, I'm upset. We need to leave tomorrow and I'm ill."

She struggled to sit up. He eased her back down.

"Now, now, can you please stay calm?"

"Yes, dear János, but only if you stop asking irritating questions."

The monks and the nun were setting up for a bloodletting.

The physician felt around her throat and her armpits.

"Have you noticed any bumps or lumps on your body?"

"Not so far."

"I'll need to check your urine."

The nun picked up a flask while the men left the room.

"I entrust you to your ladies. Ladies, please gather as much urine as possible."

They lifted Agatha from the bed. Too weak to stand on her own, one lady held up her bed gown, two others steadied her, and the nun positioned the bottle between her legs. A thin stream of urine dribbled down her leg, too little for the nun to capture.

"Will you try again, my lady? Breathe deeply."

Agatha groaned and tried again. Now the urine flowed so heavily that the nun dodged the flask around to catch the stream.

They somehow captured a flask of urine for the doctor. He examined it, looking quizzically at its yellow color.

"Well done."

He said no more, but deftly sliced open Agatha's vein. Her pallor went from green to gray as the blood drained from her body.

The physician looked up.

"The air is very stiff in here. Ladies, bring in some bells to loosen it. Agatha, dear, sip some of this wormwood syrup."

She took a swallow, gagged and vomited brown bile.

"Please try again, for the wormwood will settle your stomach. Here, chew some mint to calm your system and freshen your spirit first."

They alternated the two herbs until Agatha whispered weakly, "My stomach is better now. Thank you, János."

The ladies-in-waiting arrived carrying small bells. They circled the room, softly ringing the bells - sounds to stimulate the air without further jarring Agatha's nerves – except, she was now too worn out to care. As she drifted off to sleep, the physician studied the flask of urine.

"What our patient needs is fewer people around her. Let her rest. Everyone out."

Agatha was groggy, but he took her hand, stroking it to waken her.

"Agatha, you and I both know what's going on. Don't you think staying here a few extra days would be worth ..."

Her eyes shot daggers at him.

"No, I don't. I will not slow down the next King of England."

Brother János patted her hand.

"Alright. I'm going to leave an herbal drink right here, just in case you decide to ... to take care of things on your own."

Pulling a flask from his robe, he poured medicine into the bedside cup.

Agatha wrinkled her nose at the smell of gin and juniper, and sank back into the goose down pillows, exhausted.

"Thank you. Now leave me."

She was visibly angry.

The priest prayed the *Pater Noster* over her and quietly slipped out.

Agatha stared at the cup. Then, with one sweep of her arm, she sent the liquid flying across the room.

CHAPTER THIRTEEN:

Feather and Stone

◡

MARGARET hadn't stayed long at her stream, but she'd taken time to memorize the greens and yellows of the grasses, to imprint upon her mind the songs of each bird, to remember the scent of Hungarian air, and to feel its earth under her feet. She had hoped against hope to see the white hart one last time, but all she'd encountered today were insects, birds and rodents. Not one deer.

She stopped in her tracks. Wait. The white hart. Bishop Ealdred. Her lie. The monastery. Her penance for the lie. Oh, no, she'd never washed the feet of a poor person, the second part of her penance! How could she have forgotten? She had to do it today, right now.

Changing direction, she ran toward the town of Mecseknádasd. She had to find a poor person quickly, because she was going to be late getting back to the castle. Again.

"Mary, Mother of Jesus, please help me find a poor person right now, and the poorer the better, because now I also carry the unconfessed sin of having forgotten to do my penance. Please, Jesus, quickly send me someone with very dirty feet so I can wash them and cleanse my soul at the same time."

Her prayer was immediately answered. In fact, later on that night Margaret would wonder why the Lord seemed more attentive in answering prayers that required the giving of herself than her petitions to receive something nice, since the latter seemed to take forever.

But at the moment she was ecstatic to come upon a small family that met her needs. The pitiful-looking mother carried a crying infant while the young father pulled a decrepit, two-wheeled cart carrying a bedraggled, old woman with no teeth. The family was shocked to happen upon this ethereal child in clean, beautiful clothing, who ran meet to them with a huge smile on her face.

"May God bless you! Please let me wash Grandmother's feet."

"Excuse me, Miss?"

"I have to - no, I want to wash her feet and I hope they're very dirty. Do you have water I can use?"

"Well, we have two small jugs. Are you ... aren't you from the castle?"

"I apologize. I forget my manners. I am Margaret of Wessex and I told a bishop a lie, so I must, with deep regret in my heart at my sin, wash the feet of a poor person. Have you a clean cloth for drying?"

"I'm sorry, princess, we don't. Heaven bless us! You're the one they call as fair as a pearl, aren't you? And sure as there's dirt under my fingernails, you are that fair."

"No one with a sin like mine hanging around her neck can be called fair. I'll dry her feet with my tunic. I suppose I should wash her feet with my tears and dry them with my hair, as the woman did in the Bible, but I don't feel any tears right now."

She involuntarily recoiled when the old woman's threadbare shoes were removed. Her cracked, filthy feet stank, and her crooked toes crossed over and under one another, their untrimmed nails curling to dig into her skin. It looked painful.

Margaret dribbled water over the gnarled mess, mindful to retain as much water as possible for the peasants to drink on their journey. Her hands shook to touch the misshapen feet; nonetheless, she gently smoothed the liquid across the skin, running her fingers in-between the crossed toes while repeating, "Forgive me Jesus, for I have committed the sin of lying." By the eighth repetition, the revulsion had left her. Margaret smiled up at the old woman, who closed her eyes at the sheer pleasure of being touched with tenderness. Margaret used the hem of her wool tunic to dab the feet dry.

"Thank you," said the man, who looked at his mother kindlier than he had in a long time.

"No," said Margaret, "I thank you. That was the sweetest penance I've ever done." She touched the old woman on the cheek, who grabbed her hand to kiss it.

Glowing with joy, she hurried along the road back to the castle. A galloping horse approached. Someone from the castle must be looking for her, she thought, fretting that she was in trouble again; however, as the rider rounded the path, she recognized him.

"Brother János, what's wrong? Who's sick?"

"Your mother. It might be something she ate." He offered an arm to hoist Margaret up onto his horse. "I'll take you back to the castle. A visit from you will do her good."

Margaret knocked quietly on her mother's door and stuck her head into the room. Agatha cracked open an eye.

"Margaret."

"What's wrong, Mother?"

"Absolutely nothing. At least, nothing that the doctor hasn't taken care of. I'll be ready to leave tomorrow morning."

But Agatha's face was the color of dirty laundry water. Doubtful about a quick recovery, Margaret kissed her cheek, gently massaged her arms, and promising to return later, rounded up her siblings.

"Cristina, Edgar. Come. We must pray for Mother in the chapel."

Cristina was upset that she'd not been allowed to see her mother.

"I told them I'd be quiet, but they still wouldn't let me in. Why did you get to see her?"

"I'm the eldest, Cristina. And it was a good sign that they didn't let you in, because it means she's not dying. So take heart. We can help her best by praying, here in front of the altar."

Edgar was worried enough about his mother's illness to obediently kneel on the hard floor between his sisters.

"Say the *Ave Maria* with me, both of you. Edgar, just say the parts you know. The Virgin Mary will hear our prayers and talk to her Son about our mother."

Together, the three children chanted in sweet treble voices: *"Ave Maria, gratia plena, Dominus tecum. Benedicta tu in mulieribus, et benedictus fructus ventris tui. Amen."*

Edgar jumped in on each "Ave Maria" and "Amen." Those were the only parts he was certain about.

After ten repetitions, Cristina interrupted with a whisper.

"How many times will we need to say it before Mary hears us, Margaret?"

"It could take one hundred times for her to know our faith is deep."

"Shall we pray louder to get her attention?"

"No, I think that would only annoy her. Let's keep going."

"Ave Maria, gratia plena, Dominus tecum. Benedicta tu in mulieribus, et benedictus fructus ventris tui. Amen."

Over and over again, they repeated the prayer.

"Edgar," said Margaret, pausing to kiss him on top of his head, "you may stop after fifty. That was number thirty-two."

Although they lost count, the girls persevered until Margaret was confident they'd performed at least one hundred repetitions. Their knees hurt from kneeling and Edgar had lain down and fallen asleep.

Cristina poked him awake. Edgar immediately began to worry.

"Did the Virgin Mary hear us, Margaret?"

"Yes, I can sense her praying right now to our Lord Jesus. Mother will improve."

Etel was waiting in the hallway.

"Girls, it's time for your English lessons, and Edgar, it's past your nap time."

Edgar protested. "I don't need one. I just woke up from praying."

Etel couldn't argue with him.

"Then we'll go through your things, choosing the toys and clothes you want to keep with you on the trip and I'll pack them in your trunk."

"Will we sleep at King Andrew's court tomorrow night?" Edgar asked.

"You need to pay more attention to your lessons, Edgar. Esztergom isn't that close," said Cristina.

"It will take five or six days, since we're moving the entire household, and most of the servants will be on foot. The remaining English embassy adds about seventy-five more people to the procession. It will be slow going."

"Why aren't we traveling up the Danube?" asked Margaret.

"It's swollen from spring rains. The water's flow is too strong against us and is highly unpredictable. At least, that's what I'm told."

As soon as Margaret completed her English lesson, she selected her most prized possessions for her personal trunk. After dinner had been eaten and her prayers said, only two more things remained to be done before climbing into bed.

First, Margaret carefully rolled her heaven-sent goose feather and the white stone from her stream inside a piece of white wool cloth she'd had the weavers make, tucking the fabric bundle inside a painted wooden box. Already inside the box lay her favorite leather pouch. She rubbed her thumb over the pouch's calf skin softness, letting the scent of the hide soothe her.

Tomorrow she'd fill it with earth from Castle Réka. That way, she'd take some of Hungary with her.

Closing the box, she said aloud, "I will come back to Mecseknádasd as soon as I'm worthy to be a nun. Then I will join the convent. In the sight of God, I vow I will come back and do that."

CHAPTER FOURTEEN:

Edward and Margaret's Escape

T HE royal family and the castle staff attended Mass that auspicious morning, as they did every morning, but on this special day of departure, the celebrant was Abbot Máté from the abbey, leaving the castle's *archchaplain* feeling demoted as the concelebrant. English and Hungarian soldiers lined the walls of the chapel, ever-alert. For now, every breath they drew was dedicated to keeping Edward safe until he reached the shores of England.

But for most of the worshippers in the crowded chapel, focusing was impossible, even for Abbot Máté. The children were excited; the servants were running checklists in their heads; the exchequer worried whether he'd collected every single debt; and Edward felt a heavy mantle of responsibility laying across his shoulders. He'd spent days deciding which royal courts he wanted to visit on the way. He needed personal relationships with Europe's leaders, to categorize friend and foe. He'd waited forty years for the throne and taking it lightly now would be a waste of a lifelong desire. It would also be disrespectful to his father, Edmund Ironside, to his Kievan mentor, Yaroslav, and to the Danish earl, Walgar, who'd risked his life to spirit two babes of the House of Wessex out of England, away from the murderous King Cnut. Edward owed Walgar his very life. He prayed for blessings upon all those who had protected him.

Almost before the final "Amen," the chapel exploded with animated conversation, while the household and soldiers waited for Edward and the family to exit the chapel first. Edward leaned over and whispered in Margaret's ear.

"What do you say we shake loose from these guards and get some fresh air? Are you up for a ride through the hills? The horses are ready to go if you are."

"Yes, yes, and yes!"

They, the tall and the small, ran to the stables, alarming Edward's guards. The soldiers' cries of "Stand aside!" were largely ignored by the chatting worshippers who eased over casually, inhibiting the soldiers' exit.

By the time they had pushed their way through the crowd into the hallway, their charge and his daughter had vanished. The guards split into groups, heading in opposite directions.

Meanwhile, the fugitives were already mounting their horses: Edward, on his magnificent white stallion and Margaret, on her chestnut *palfrey* with the soft mouth and the powerful hindquarters.

"Where to, Father?" Margaret asked.

"I'll follow you. I long to remember what freedom smells like!"

Margaret took the lead, flying up and down rolling hills, her father following on her heels, laughing in exhilaration. Margaret felt it too. She threw her head back and let out an Anglo-Saxon war cry her father had taught her, "Ut, Ut!"

Out! Out!

They rode as though astride Pegasus', until both humans and beasts tired, finally ambling toward a small stream. Dismounting, father and daughter allowed the sweating horses to wade into its coolness.

Margaret knelt at the bank, cupping her hands to scoop up cold water.

"Your hair is getting wet," Edward cautioned. "Pull it back before you're soaked."

"Good!" said Margaret, pounding her fists into the water to drench herself.

"Well, well. A warrior lives inside my delicate princess."

"The warrior doesn't show up very often."

"Then, remember that she's there. You'll find her useful in your life."

Shouting and the pounding hooves of horses were approaching in the distance. The guards had found them.

Edward cocked his head.

"Is the warrior prepared to race them back to the castle?"

"Yes, she is."

"Let's go, then."

He boosted his daughter onto her horse, and they took off, Edward leading them into a shallow gulley, where they dropped from sight of the guards.

"This way," he said, reining hard to the left. "We'll circle behind them while they're coming this way."

"Olicross!" shouted Margaret, calling on the Holy Cross to help them evade their handlers.

The guards didn't stand a chance.

To her chagrin, Margaret's inner warrior dissipated in a vat of self-pity when the children stood in their bed chamber for the final time.

"We must say goodbye to our childhood," announced Margaret, still damp from the stream.

"Even me?" whined Edgar.

"Yes," replied Margaret. "Look at the wooden sword in your hand. You're learning the art of war. By the time Father is coronated, you'll be a tiny soldier."

"I'm going to protect him when he's king."

"What will I do when I'm grown?" asked Cristina.

"You and I will come back to Násdad and be nuns at Pécsvárad Monastery. Won't that be wonderful?"

"Maybe, unless I find a boy who thinks I'm prettier than you. And if he's a king, I'll definitely marry him. Yes, that will work, because once Father is king, I'll be more … what's that word, Margaret?"

"You'll be more 'eligible,' Cristina."

"Eligible, that's it. But if I don't find a king, then I'll be a nun with you. But I'd rather marry. Don't you want to marry a king, even a little bit?"

"No. I want to be the bride of Christ and live at the abbey."

"I don't understand you, Margaret."

"Me, neither," piped up Edgar.

"You don't understand anything, Edgar," said Cristina. "How will you ever be king?"

"Edgar will be a man before we know it. Mother says we're all growing up before she's ready," Margaret said, gazing out her little window for the last time. Today, everything was for the last time, and she hated it. Even when she came back in a few years, it wouldn't be exactly the same. Just as her stream continually changed as the water flowed over its rocks, the abbey would be different when she returned. But return she would.

The sound of whinnying horses floated into the room. The Hungarian household and the remaining Englishmen were lining up in the procession order. Edgar nearly exploded with excitement.

"Let's go! I want to watch."

"Yes, let's go," said Cristina. "And I'm not saying goodbye to my childhood."

"Me, neither," said Edgar, relieved.

Cristina grabbed his hand to run outside.

Margaret stayed behind, watching the rays of pale sunrise glide across the floor toward the opposite wall. She mourned the moon she'd not see through this window again. It wouldn't be the same moon in England. How could it be? Hers was a silvery, tender, and forgiving Mother Moon that had shone full on the night she was born. Just as people spoke different languages in different countries, she was certain that the moon whispered differently into one's heart in foreign countries.

Her hand brushed against the Gospel-book she'd attached to her tunic with a silk sling. She'd kept the volume close since the day she'd received it. It was light and would fit in the palm of her hand once she was fully grown. It was her forever link to Pécsvárad Abbey. She opened to the book of Mark. The first page was lavishly illuminated with the Evangelist sitting at a table, a Gospel-book in one hand and a pen in the other. She ran her finger over the gold illumination and guessed at what the Lord was telling her: that He would give her strength if she read these gospels, and if she had faith. But she didn't feel any faith right now, so for today she'd try and let faith live in her head and hope it found its way back into her heart someday soon.

She turned and followed her siblings outside.

The air was filled with as much chatter as clatter. The nobles, religious, clerks, and soldiers, whether English or Hungarian; peasants, servants, ladies, whether old or young, excited or nostalgic, were resplendent in their brand new clothes, and many were already mounted up, the men astride and many Hungarian women riding side saddle so their lovely new dresses cascaded down the side of their horse. Edward's most prized horses, stallions and mares, were lined up, each magnificent *palfrey* and *destrier* overseen by its own groom and a guard dog. Knights and nobles each brought along several horses. Then there were the mules and poor packhorses, condemned by their sturdy builds to pull the loaded four-wheel wagons.

These large wooden wagons were girded with iron ribs and topped by brightly painted fabric canopies. The wagons transporting people were also stocked with pillows, rugs, personal trunks and built-in benches.

Moving the kitchen, from knives to pots - required four wagons, a team of five horses each, the driver, and a guard dog.

The royal court's treasury wagon was assigned two dogs and four soldiers, since an entourage this large would certainly attract the attention of robbers.

Many carts were packed with bedding and clothing; others carried food and wine for the company. Stopping at castles, monasteries, or hunting lodges at night, it was still prudent to be partially self-sustaining, so coming along were farm animals: chickens, cows, goats, and sheep. The party could hunt along the way for wild game; to that end, one large wagon contained nothing but cages of hooded falcons, followed by another carrying the castle's exclusively-bred hunting dogs.

Edward had designated that his personal wagons, with extra thick wooden sides, and reinforced with iron locks and extra iron ribbing, would carry the altar ornaments, crucifixes, sacred vessels, liturgical books and costly priestly vestments. They were pulled by five sturdy horses with several guards. Another of his other wagons was reserved for his personal fortune: trunks purposely made too heavy for robbers to carry away easily, some of them secured by a puzzle of locks protecting the gold and silver, jewelry, books, artwork, tapestries, crowns, clothing, and, most precious of all, his holy relics, including a piece of the true cross given to him by Yaroslav in Kiev. Soldiers and a cadre of dogs encircled the wagons. Edward and his treasures would be watched every moment of the trip by trusted, watchful eyes.

Several chariots were stacked with barrels of Hungarian wine and regional products, gifts to please royal hosts.

Edward's stallion waited for his master with majestic still-ness, standing near the end of the procession, attended by his personal groom, and surrounded by mounted knights. Edward and Agatha wouldn't proceed outside until the last moment.

First off today, they would parade through the town of Mecseknádasd, so the proud villagers could say goodbye to their former exile and wish the family well. Peasants and *thegns* alike were thrilled by the prospect of knowing a future king.

Margaret had never participated in one of these parades, but they sounded pleasant enough. She'd hoped to ride on her horse through the town, but their mother was not well enough to ride, so instead, the girls would stay with her inside the most lavish of all the wagons. They planned to hold open the heavy fabric window flaps, so the people could see the future queen wave farewell to them.

One of the English knights volunteered to share his mount with Edgar. The boy already had his wooden sword out of its scabbard, prepared to defend his father from any and all unknown dangers. The adults found him adorable.

A young page with dark hair strolled by Margaret. She recognized him as the boy from the great hall the night of the Ealdred's announcement, and the boy Cristina had swooned over. Margaret called to her sister.

"Cristina, I believe this page has offered to take care of our needs. Will you supervise him?"

Cristina looked thrilled and could barely catch her breath. Margaret was relieved to see that her sister tripped only once on her way over, because she became quite clumsy when excited. The boy bowed to her. Cristina could barely talk.

"Of course, I can supervise him, Margaret," she managed to squeeze out. Her heart was racing, her head was spinning, and her thoughts were stitched together as unevenly as her embroidery. But she quickly came up with instructions for the boy that would keep him nearby.

"You must always stay close to me ... I ... I mean, we will need you to ride alongside all of us ... to the side of our wagon, and within earshot. Mother is not feeling well, and we will require a strong page like yourself to guard her ... and, to keep all of us safe."

He bowed again. "Yes, Milady."

Margaret prayed that Cristina wouldn't collapse into a heap at his feet.

He bowed to leave.

"Wait," said Cristina, suddenly recovering. "I don't know your name."

"My name is Pál."

As Cristina and Pál commenced some exploratory flirting, Margaret wandered away, strolling along a strand of trees that lined the road in front of the castle. Trying to appear casual, she pulled the leather pouch from inside her tunic, casually scanning the ground for loose dirt. She found some and scooped up a handful of her homeland, shoving it into the pouch, and knotting the leather strings so that no Hungarian soil would spill on the journey.

She hoped no one had seen her.

But someone had. Unwin leaned against a nearby chariot, his eyes fixated on her. She tried scowling at him but couldn't meet his unblinking gaze. As angry as she was at herself for being weak, he continued to unnerve her. Securing the pouch on her belt, she walked in the opposite direction, toward the family wagon, where she'd feel safer.

CHAPTER FIFTEEN:

The Heartbeat of Change

𝔄 MATTRESS and blankets were waiting inside the wagon for Agatha, with piles of pillows scattered along the built-in wooden bench for Margaret, Cristina, Edgar and Nursemaid Etel. Margaret checked inside her personal trunk. Yes, her box containing the feather and the white pebble was safe. She added the pouch of dirt to the box and snapped it closed, hiding her treasure box in-between layers of clothing.

Edward's guards walked out of the castle in tight formation, lining both sides of the bridge over the castle's ditch and standing at attention as Edward and Agatha emerged from the castle to rousing cheers. Margaret hurried to open the cart's flap and watched her mother, who looked regal, if pale. She was leaning heavily on Edward's arm, although she tried not to show it. She smiled and waved, but Margaret saw the fatigue deep in her eyes and how heavy her legs must have felt. Edward guided her up the steps of the wagon into the arms of her ladies-in-waiting. They quickly pulled the wagon's flap closed so they could ease Agatha onto the wool-stuffed mattress. She closed her eyes, sighed and collapsed in a heap.

A heart-broken Margaret took her mother's hand. They were leaving behind everything familiar for a faraway foreign country. It was too much for her sick mother to handle. She was

[handwritten margin note: not done, but okay]

surprised when her mother spoke firmly to her, as if she'd read Margaret's mind.

"Hear me, Margaret. Health and sickness, birth and death, sunset or sunrise, leaving and arriving - any change in your life lasts but a couple of heartbeats, because life moves on, with or without you. You can't control it - easier to pick up a raindrop with your fingers than to control God's will."

"Yes, Mother," she answered.

From the back of the procession came a commanding shout – it was her father, ordering the procession to commence the journey. Their move to a new life was beginning. Margaret could hardly bear to look.

Cristina lifted a window flap to see if Pál had stayed close by. When she saw that he was riding closely alongside the wagon, she let out a little squeal. Thank God, thought Margaret. Cristina had found a boy.

The caravan turned east onto a Roman road, one of the ancient roads built wide enough to accommodate larger vehicles. The wooden wheels of Agatha's wagon slipped and thumped over the deep ruts engraved in the stones over many years. Her face was soon bathed in sweat.

"Get me some fresh air, Margaret. I can't be dripping with sweat when we ride through the village."

Margaret threw open the flaps and fanned her mother's face.

Agatha grabbed the bowl next to her mattress, throwing up violently and terrifying Cristina.

"What is it, Mother? Is it the pox? Please don't die!"

"These bumpy roads are not good for you," fretted Margaret.

"I will rest at King Andrew's court. Edward plans to stay a while."

"But what if this kills you before we get to Esztergom?"

Cristina's lower lip quivered.

"Oh, heavens, Cristina," answered Agatha.

Thankfully, the town of Mecseknádasd was only three miles away. Even before they reached town, the road was lined with well-wishers. It seemed that everyone had turned out to see Edward off to England: nobles, clergy, farmers, blacksmiths, bowl makers, sheep herders - skilled craftsmen and unskilled peasants, alike.

Margaret wiped her mother's brow, helping her sit up and wave. Agatha was beloved in Nasdad, and she received much cheering, paling only compared to the wild exulting Edward received. Older villagers remembered the day when two exiled brothers had arrived from Kiev, riding into town behind the newly crowned King Andrew. The handsome young princes had embraced this country and the villagers felt they had a stake in Edward's grand future. He had always been fair to them and considerate of their welfare. They were sorry to see him leave, but their pride outweighed their sentimentality.

As the procession entered the heart of town, Margaret saw lines of clergy, monks, priests and nuns from the monastery, waiting to add their own farewells. She was delighted to see Abbess Anna Mária standing along the road, waving, clapping and shouting encouragement to the family like an enthusiastic novice.

Margaret searched both sides of the road for Ludmila. She desperately wanted to say farewell to her friend. Margaret couldn't find her anywhere. She called out to the Abbess.

"Please tell dear Ludmila goodbye for me."

Anna Mária just smiled and waved, nodding.

Margaret sank back, slumping against a pillow, looking out the back of the wagon.

Agatha, too ill to mince words, reminded her crisply, "God's will never lies behind us, Margaret. Turn around and look forward."

At the outskirts of the town, the crowd thinned and disappeared. The procession turned north. Hopefully there would be good roads ahead, and decent rivers to ford.

The caravan went quiet as people contemplated the journey ahead. The show was over for now. It was time to stay alert for bandits, wild animals and bad weather.

Agatha slowly chewed a piece of bread, while the girls and Etel ate cheese.

Margaret thought she heard someone say her name.

"Do you hear that?" she asked.

"Yes," said Cristina. "Someone is calling for you."

"Margaret! Margaret!"

The voice was coming closer, clearly heard over the grinding of wheels on rock.

Cristina peered out the window.

"Margaret, take a look. You won't believe your eyes."

Margaret peeked out the back flap.

"Mother!" she laughed. "Sometimes God's will does lie behind us!"

"Who is it?"

"It's Ludmila, come to say goodbye. Over here, Ludmila!"

Ludmila rode up on a broken-down packhorse. They were both out of breath by the time she pulled up alongside the wagon. Margaret reached out to touch her.

"Thank you for coming to say goodbye. I'm going to miss you so much."

"You don't have to say goodbye. Not yet, anyway. It's a miracle, Margaret. Abbess Anna Mária just gave me permission to ride with the embassy to King Andrew's court and to stay with you until you leave there."

Margaret was ecstatic. "May the Lord bless her forever. Oh, Ludmila! Come, we'll make room for you inside the wagon."

"Not unless they hitch up another horse to pull my heft. No, I'll ride this old nag. Poor girl, her knees are ready to give out. I'll see you at sunset, when the procession stops. Oh, Margaret, I'm so happy."

"Not any happier than I am," said Margaret, whose smile burst like sun through clouds.

CHAPTER SIXTEEN:

Margaret Blunders

THEY didn't get as far as expected on the first day. Agatha's condition required rest stops along the way, so they'd had to halt short of the castle at which they'd planned on staying. Instead, they would stay at the smaller castle of a *thegn*.

To quickly accommodate the unexpected caravan, a large fire had been built in front of the residence, where the party digested their dinner and chatted. Margaret and Ludmila sat close to the flames in carved wooden chairs. Margaret, more delicate than most, was cold, so Ludmila wrapped her in a thick wool blanket. Both girls were stuffed from dinner. The rather minor local lord had fed them nearly everything he had on hand: mutton, hedgehog, porcupine, and some venison, supplemented with vegetables and bread and fruit. The meat had been plentiful: the nobleman desperately sought to impress the future king, even though he knew the animals he'd slaughtered early would be missed come winter. For Margaret's family, it wasn't exactly a feast, but eating well without having to sneak extra food had Ludmila marveling at her good fortune.

"That tasted so good, Margaret. I'll remember tonight's meal forever, but I fear I've committed the sin of gluttony. Worms are going to feast on my flesh in hell."

Despite the gruesome thought of hell, her joy in Ludmila's presence made everything amusing for Margaret. Even hell.

"When was the last time you feasted, Ludmila? If I were to bet, which is a sin so I won't, but if I did, I'd bet you can't even remember. Besides, today is Sunday, the Lord's day, when we are supposed to enjoy Him, and don't forget the charity you perform by being with me, so do penance if you wish, but I bless the Lord for your company tonight."

They ruminated in contentment, thinking their own thoughts. Margaret leaned in, whispering in a conspiratorial tone, "Besides, I noted how fast Abbot Máté downed his dinner. After he consumed the deer liver and tongues, I'm sure I caught him eyeing the antlers in case they were edible."

Ludmila caught her rising guffaw in her hand.

"Margaret of Wessex, I'm shocked. You're like my little sister and I've never heard you speak that way. Now I like you even better than before."

"It's your fault, Ludmila. You bring out my wickedness."

"The devil doesn't even know what you look like, Margaret. He'll burn my soul to a crisp long before he knows you exist."

"We'll see. I do think our prayers for Mother are working. I saw her eat some fruit tonight."

"Did she? That's encouraging."

Ludmila squinted at something behind Margaret and spoke softly.

"Margaret. Don't turn around, but there's a man watching you. I saw him staring at you earlier today. I didn't want to say anything."

Margaret swallowed hard.

"Does he have greasy hair and pocked skin?"

"He looks like he fell into a pot of sizzling oil and was pecked by the frying hens."

"Is he a soldier?"

"Are they allowed to be so ugly?"

"When he looks at you, do you feel like flies are crawling all over you?"

"Yes! He's one of Satan's minions, isn't he? He's most likely possessed by the demons of paganism. Abbot Máté can perform an exorcism. I'll fetch him."

"Please don't. The man's name is Unwin and he's an archer. Bishop Ealdred knew him by name. I was sure he would travel to Jerusalem with the bishop, but I guess he didn't."

"Tell your father to get rid of him. He's evil."

"Father is too busy, and the guards make it impossible to get to him, anyway."

"I'm going to walk right past those chain mail idiots and talk to your father."

Margaret was horrified.

"No, you will not! Ludmila. You haven't the bloodline to confront an heir to the throne."

It was a stinging rebuke, uncharacteristic of Margaret, who longed to take it back even as the words spilled from her mouth.

Ludmila's ample frame shrunk before Margaret's eyes. She was stunned, and Margaret was horrified at what she'd done to her friend.

"I'm sorry, Ludmila."

"No, Princess, you're right. It's not my place."

"Please don't call me Princess."

"But you are."

"Not yet, and we are all equal in God's gaze."

"I'll never wear a crown, Margaret."

"Maybe in heaven."

"Of course, when a cockroach sits at the Father's right hand."

"You're an angel, Ludmila."

"There's not a person at the abbey who would agree with you."

They shared a weak laugh, then stared uncomfortably into the fire, pretending their friendship hadn't just been ravaged.

Once it was dark, most of the royals, the upper-class members of the party, along with the two abbots, Alwyn and Máté, headed inside the *thegn's* castle to find their accommodations for the night. Had this been one of the planned stops, their rooms would have been more luxurious, but as it stood, the rest of the religious, including Ludmila, would sleep in the village churches. The servants would sleep in the loaded wagons while the soldiers stood guard against roving bandits.

Edgar bounded up to the girls, his newest wooden sword in hand. He was far from tired. He tapped Ludmila on the shoulder with the point of the blade.

"Sister, Cristina is talking honey to some boy and Margaret's no fun, so will you please come and play with me?"

Now it was Margaret's turn to feel hurt. She tried to explain.

"I'm sorry, Edgar. Playing isn't something I'm good at."

Ludmila jumped up, relieved to escape the emotional chasm between her and Margaret.

"Lucky for you, young man, I'm very good at playing. The nuns have decided that fun is my gift from God, since it's all I'm good at. So, run, boy, run, before I steal your sword and carve you into tiny pieces!"

Edgar dashed off to run in circles, giggling uncontrollably. Ludmila couldn't keep up with him, but she could outsmart him. Ambushed at every turn, his gleeful squeals were a painful reminder to Margaret of her sisterly inadequacies. No one observing her sweet face could have guessed at the depressing self-image Margaret was concocting. They would have laughed at her forlorn self-incrimination, but she was caught in its grip.

What a dreary girl I am, she thought. And cruel. I'm a dreary and cruel girl. And my faith is too weak to become a nun. I'm dreary and cruel and weak and I'll be dreadfully and eternally punished for my sins, if not now, then on Judgment Day.

She studied her reflection in her silver cup. It was a grim sight, as though someone had written across her forehead: You've hurt your best friend's feelings; your little brother avoids you because you're no fun; and your faith has fallen through a sieve because the Lord has called your father to be king of England.

She sighed and thought to herself, even I don't want to be with me.

So where did that leave her? Ludmila would never wear the beautiful clothing like Margaret would, yet she'd be welcomed into heaven because she was a sweet and simple soul; Cristina was learning how to flirt and would happily marry one day; and somehow, adorable, spoiled, playful Edgar would grow up to sit on a throne.

But her own sins felt overwhelming. She'd been haughty tonight. Earlier in the evening, when someone had called her beautiful, she had swelled with pride. Now she remembered from the Old Testament of the *bibliotheca* that pride went before destruction and being haughty before a fall. She'd have to avoid pride in her looks and satisfaction in her royal blood at all costs. If she could manage that, she might still have a chance for redemption.

Margaret stood and stretched, pulling the blanket tightly around her neck, pretending that someone had temporarily stepped away and would return at any moment. She watched the clumps of people gossiping. She was no good at that either, but she decided she didn't want to be good at gossip. That was one bright spot.

She moped her way around the camp, waving at Ludmila, who was too busy chasing Edgar, laughing and shouting, to notice. Margaret plastered a fake smile on her face but couldn't concentrate enough to hold it in place.

The day was dying in concert with Margaret's spirits and the fire's light was too bright for a girl who longed for the darkness to match her pitiful mood. She wandered away, drawn to the edge of a nearby forest.

A pomegranate sun quivered over the horizon, barely shedding sufficient light for her to see her way. She was uncaring when her blanket caught on spindly bush branches; the thick stand of trees beyond was calling to her. Perhaps she'd discover a stream there from which the trees drank. Nature always guided her toward joy.

As soon as the trees swallowed her up and the fire disappeared from view, she fell on her knees to pray.

"... my cup runs over ..." She heard a noise and paused, then her heart leapt: someone was coming toward her, snapping twigs along the way, making sounds exactly like those Ludmila had made the day she'd found her in the forest and taken her to the abbey. Obviously, her friend had forgiven her and was coming to salve her despair! Jubilation flooded her heart.

But a nasty snort made Margaret freeze. She recognized the distinct sound of a wild pig. She turned around slowly. It had swollen teats. With rising panic, she realized she must be standing between this sow and her litter. Margaret raised her arms over her head, trying to look larger, as she slowly backed away, but the pig was undeterred and readied a charge. Margaret was in trouble and the only prayer she could think of was, "Lord, have mercy." She wanted to call for help but couldn't force breath into the scream that clogged her throat.

Thud. The sow hesitated, confused. It shook its head and wobbled, but focused again on Margaret, who was considering climbing the tree she'd just backed into; however, she knew that wild pigs were jumpers. Like a bear, the sow could and would pull her down faster than she could climb, crushing the bones of whatever limb those jaws clamped onto.

Thud. This time she saw an arrow hit the animal. It emitted an angry scream that split the fading light. The sow's front legs crumpled, and she sank slowly to the ground in front of

Margaret, life spurting from its side. Margaret leaped away from the growing red pool of blood and looked around.

Who had saved her?

"Thank you. Whoever you are, thank you. Please come out so I can see you."

A middle-aged man shuffled into the clearing, looking more embarrassed than triumphant, his eyes avoiding hers, his bow already strung with a third arrow.

Margaret was shocked. Of all the people on earth, it was Unwin.

"You! I mean, thank you, Unwin. But …"

Words failed her. She was shocked by her hero's identity, and his presence upset her even more so now, because he had saved her from harm, maybe even from death, and within the hour she'd spoken ill of him. It was another blot of sin against her.

Unwin mumbled something. She encouraged him in a shaky voice. Her heart was still pounding.

"Please speak up. And speak slowly so I can understand your English."

"I know you don't like me," he stammered, "because I drink too much and when I do, I'm rude. And I know … I know you see me staring at you. But my orders are …"

His voice deflated itself of air; he stared at the sky. Was this a hardened warrior or a repentant boy standing in front of her?

"I don't understand, Unwin."

He blurted it out.

"Miss, I'm your bodyguard. My orders are to protect you. That's why I watch you. You weren't supposed to find out, but I didn't do a very good job of keeping it secret."

"Who in the world made you my protector?"

"Your father."

"My father?"

"I'm very good with bow and arrow, Miss, and when I don't drink too much, I can track prey with the best of them."

Margaret tried to think of something that sounded grateful. She was still in shock.

"Well, then, thank you for not drinking too much tonight."

She looked down at the dead sow and felt sorry for her babies, but she was grateful to be unhurt, and she knew the piglets wouldn't go to waste.

Someday, she thought, I going to have to forgive Unwin for his horrible behavior the first time we met. But not today.

She was interrupted by her father's voice.

"Unwin, are you with her? Is all well?"

"Over here, Sire."

Edward burst into the clearing, followed by his guards. He hurried to Margaret, hugging her tightly to his chest.

"Thank you, Jesus. All praise to the Father."

He stepped back to examine her.

"You're not hurt? Are you sure you're not bleeding?"

"I'm not at all hurt, thanks to Unwin."

Edward pulled her in close again, whispering urgently in her ear.

"I know the man frightens you. I know what happened that first day because he confessed it to me, but Margaret, he's not really like that, and you need him. We live in constant danger now, like chess pieces in real life. From now on, before you make a move, consider its consequences. Promise me you'll begin to think like a queen."

"I promise. I'm so ashamed. I've learned my lesson this time."

CHAPTER SEVENTEEN:

Humility

---

*T*HE trip north to Esztergom should have been an unremarkable undertaking. The route was frequently traveled by traders, noblemen and messengers coming from the king's court. Other than the threat of wild animals, of which Margaret was now keenly aware, and the ever-present possibility of robbers, most of the difficulties on this trip were expected to be mundane: a lame horse, those ubiquitous pot holes in the ancient Roman roads made more shoddy by each use and swollen rivers that couldn't safely be forded.

But Agatha's mysterious malady had changed everything. The company halted several times a day to give her respite. She'd thrown up so many times over the last four days that no number of herbs or loosened canvas coverings mitigated the wagon's stench. The doctor and ladies-in-waiting who attended Agatha, pressed rosemary-soaked linen to their noses. Margaret now rode her horse most of the time to escape the smell, while Cristina and Edgar preferred riding in a two-wheeled chariot.

Now they'd stopped again. Arrival at King Andrew's court would be delayed another day because of the slow pace, but more troublesome, the party still wasn't moving fast enough to reach the usual manorial castles at which nobles liked to spend the night. Instead, for the last few days, scouts had ridden ahead, scrambling to find monasteries or estates large enough to provide any accommodations. The nobles secretly grumbled.

Edward convened a meeting on horseback with the senior English nobles. After a brief discussion, the men shook hands and the Englishmen rode the length of the party, shouting to their countrymen.

The English embassy would go ahead, minus those required for security of the royal family. They would try fording the river, if it weren't running too fast, and make their own grand entrance into Esztergom, or find a nice place to stay and wait outside the city for the Hungarian embassy to join them. Edward's party would get there as soon as possible.

The English chose the first option, departing hastily, relieved to pick up the pace and lessen their time on the road.

Margaret took advantage of the thinning ranks to search for Ludmila. She found her in the middle of the party, plodding along on another broken-down packhorse.

"Oh, no. We must find you a better horse. This one has two hooves in the grave."

"I'm fine, really, Princess."

"There you go, calling me by that horrid title. Well, then, let me see. Since I at least will be a princess, I can command you to call me Margaret, can't I?"

"I'm guessing you can."

"Then I command you to do so. Please." Her lip quivered. "But that doesn't really help, because I can't command you to love me." She reined her horse to a stop. "So, I'm begging you to be my friend. I hardly have any, so please, Ludmila. Forgive me my sinful pride and be my friend again."

They both sniffed and hugged, reaching across their horses with fervent promises of eternal sisterhood. Ludmila wiped away Margaret's tears and brushed back a tear-soaked strand of hair trailing down her own cheek.

Margaret wiped her nose with a silk handkerchief. She nodded toward someone standing behind Ludmila's horse.

"Turn around and look."

Unwin stood nearby, partially hidden behind a tree, watching them intently, suspicion written across his face, trying to ascertain whether Margaret was in danger. Ludmila saw him scrutinizing her and burst out laughing. She waved to him.

"Hello, Unwin. I'm not a dangerous sow, although I may look like one!"

Margaret reassured him, too.

"I'm fine, Unwin."

He doffed his cap shyly.

Ludmila was surprised.

"Don't tell me you're friends with the man now!"

"Not exactly friends, but you know, when he doesn't drink too much ale, he's very good at saving my life."

"I heard. I wanted to follow your father to make sure you were all right, but I feared you didn't want me there."

"Just the opposite! You won't believe this, and I hope it doesn't hurt your feelings because I don't want to lose you again, but when I first heard the pig behind me, I thought it was you coming to find me, and I was so happy that you'd forgiven me."

Ludmila laughed.

"Anyone could make that mistake. Only Jesus can tell the difference between me and a wild pig coming through the woods. And if I learn how to snort, I might be able to fool even Him."

"You're so humble, my Ludmila. Let me be your student. Teach me humility. I have an idea, let's switch horses. It will be my first lesson in humility. You ride my *palfrey* and I'll ride whatever that four-legged dead thing is you're riding."

Ludmila was horrified, but Margaret insisted. Riding the nag turned out to be more comfortable than Margaret expected. Despite the bony shoulders, its sway-backed gait nearly rocked her to sleep. Humility wasn't so difficult, after all.

The sight of beautiful Margaret on a nag drew stares, but no one dared say anything, except for Abbot Máté, who wedged his horse in-between the two girls for an explanation.

"Sister Ludmila, what do we have here?"

Margaret quickly interceded on Ludmila's behalf.

"Dear Abbot Máté, this was my idea. Ludmila, at my request, is teaching me about humility. Isn't that charitable of her?"

"It's neither charitable nor suitable, Margaret."

"Didn't our Lord ride into Jerusalem on an ass? This decrepit packhorse is my pitiful attempt to emulate our Lord."

The abbot ignored her and turned to the trembling Ludmila.

"You will confess your pride and lack of wisdom after Mass, sister. Dismount, both of you. Margaret, you obviously require education about humility and charity. Are you reading your Gospel-book every night?"

"Well, not since we left the castle," Margaret replied, looking guilty. "My personal belongings are in mother's wagon and she's been so very sick …"

"Sister Ludmila, the first part of your penance is to retrieve Margaret's personal Gospel-book and bring it to her. Go now, girl. As for you, Margaret, when the Lord Jesus rode into Jerusalem on a donkey, he was making a statement as the Son of God. You have no need to make that statement."

"But, dear abbot, don't we strive to be worthy of our reward in heaven by being humble? And did He not teach that we are all equal in the eyes of God?"

"Are you questioning my theology?"

"No, no Your Grace. Please forgive me."

She reached for his hand and kissed it.

"You are a stubborn child. Yes, He treasures our souls equally, but our destinies on earth are different. St. Paul is very clear in 1 Corinthians that each of us manifests some gift from Him. So, while we are all part of His body, we are not all the same part. You are a diadem in His crown. Ludmila is a little toe nail, convenient to have, but unbidden to shine. Her destiny is without the glory of great deeds or great beauty. Here on earth, you and a lay sister are not equal. I will beat that message into Ludmila, if I must."

"Please, Abbot Máté, no beatings, there are much worse sinners in this caravan than Ludmila. Let me instruct her. Please see if I understand your teaching: I was born into royalty, not of my own doing, but of the Lord's will. Had He wanted Ludmila to wear a crown, He would have given her a different birth. Do I understand your valuable lesson?"

"I hope so."

"Then I shall teach her. But I may love Ludmila as deeply as the Lord loves her, am I also correct?"

"Yes, but only on a specific level, one befitting your station."

Margaret was bewildered. She didn't understand all these categories of love. Why did the clergy confound her so often?

"Thank you, Abbot Máté, for the lesson. I think understand better now, and I praise Him that you've taught me how humility works."

"Good. Come to me with any further questions, Margaret."

"Of course, I will, good abbot. Thank you."

Margaret watched him ride away, frowning. She glanced at Unwin and made a face. He looked concerned.

"Are you alright?"

"I don't think you can save me from this, Unwin. When I pray, thoughts come to me, and sometimes the clergy says things that don't fit with what I hear by the stream."

She'd have to think about it later. Perhaps, at the age of eleven, she was too young to understand. Maybe she would understand when she was twelve.

Unwin shrugged. "The abbot is right. Everything is God's will. We're equal in His eyes, but not equal here on earth."

"I guess it's possible ... wait, so you're not a pagan?"

"Of course not, Miss. I'm a baptized Christian, and sort of the bishop's secret weapon. Oh, I get in trouble with my drinking, but he knows I'm a faithful servant of God and better yet, that my aim is sure and that I can string the bow quickly."

"Perhaps I've misjudged you, Unwin."

He grinned, nervously pulling his cap over his ears.

"That's alright. I deserve it."

Ludmila came hurrying back to Margaret as fast as she could.

"Is the abbot going to punish me with a beating?"

"No, I wouldn't let him, Ludmila."

Ludmila mounted her horse, relieved.

"Jesus, have mercy. Thank you, Lord. And thank you, Margaret." She handed Margaret her box of personal items. "But I have bad news. You must go see your mother. She's very sick."

"But they told me she was getting stronger."

"If this is stronger, she must have been near death before. She doesn't look good, Margaret."

"Are they bleeding her too often?"

"They're not bleeding her at all."

"What? Isn't Brother János taking care of her?"

"They say he visits her only once a day, because there's nothing he can do for her malady."

"But, what's wrong with her? No one seems to know!"

A chill gripped Margaret's heart. The demons were laughing at her. She whirled her horse around and headed for the wagon.

The smell of vomit and the grinding sound of retching greeted her before she even dropped her horse's reins on the ground.

A nun and two ladies-in-waiting were keeping vigil with Agatha, wiping the sweat from her brow and coaxing her to sip a concoction of mint, chamomile and borage.

Margaret looked quizzically at the attendants. Her mother's eyes were closed. A nun wiped drops of bile from her lips.

"Mother?"

Agatha's eyes barely opened. She smiled faintly.

"You shouldn't have come. I don't want you to see me like this."

"I need to be with you when you're in trouble. How can I help? Brother János should be doing more to take care of you? Please tell me that you're not … you're not …"

"No, I'm not dying. You must believe me. Just pray for me. I'll get better."

"How do you know that, Mother? Do you know what's wrong with you?"

"Yes, my love. I'll explain when it's time."

Shouts rang out to mount up. The company was on the move again. Agatha's rest was over. She let out a moan as the wagon began to sway. Margaret refused to leave her side. She sat, holding a rosemary-scented cloth to her nose with one hand, and Agatha's hand in the other, until the company reached a monastery at which they'd spend the night.

CHAPTER EIGHTEEN:

Joy Presumed

𝔄S soon as they arrived, Agatha was carried on a litter into the best bedroom at the monastery, where the floors were strewn with the restful scents of chamomile and lavender and the nuns brought in trays of food to stimulate her appetite. Downstairs, the rest of the traveling party savored yet another local feast. Each guest was served a whole chicken, followed by thick slabs of pork and vegetables, all washed down with ale and wine. Dates, piled like mountains on wooden trays, arrived for dessert.

A lady-in-waiting tapped Edward on the shoulder, curtsied and whispered something in his ear. He asked her a question and she shook her head, no. Edward excused himself and left for Agatha's room, where her dinner sat untouched.

"I need your opinion, Agatha. If we push hard tomorrow, we can reach the outskirts of Esztergom. But if we stay here for a few days, you'll be able to recover your strength, which is more important to me. I'm worried that you haven't eaten in two days."

"My opinion is that you should hurry to Andrew's side. I'm slowing you down, Edward, and that's not acceptable. I'll stay here for a few days and then join you."

"I'll not leave my best advisor and wife behind. No, I won't enter the city without you beside me. It's only fitting."

Agatha mustered the strength to sit up, sipping water from the cup he offered her.

"Then I say we push to Esztergom's limits, but allow a day for my ladies to clean me, wash my hair and ply me with potions until I appear respectable. I'll ride up to the king's front door with you, even if you have to tie me to my horse."

"You are braver than my strongest knight." He reached into his pouch. "I brought you some dates. Will you eat one to seal our agreement? It would please me."

Agatha nibbled at it.

"It tastes good, my darling Edward. I only pray it tastes equally as good when it comes right back up."

"My lady, if you keep it down, you'll make me the happiest man alive." He placed two more dates into her hand. "Here - think of the Trinity - one for the Father, the second for the Son and the third for the Holy Ghost."

"Pray that I can keep the Trinity down, for if I can, I'll be on that horse in two days."

"We will pray for you at Mass. You are more beloved than I, it seems."

"If my stomach weren't so sore, I'd laugh."

She laid back down, clutching the dates.

"I'll eat these before the sun rises, I promise."

"You've always kept your promises, Agatha."

"It's the best gift I can give you, Edward."

"Getting well would be another welcome gift."

"You'll have it."

She took another bite and urged him to return to the great hall.

Not long after, Agatha was awakened by another knock. Margaret entered with her box of personal items tucked under her arm.

"Mother, you've eaten nearly half a date!"

"Actually, I've eaten one and a half dates. That would be the Father and half of the Son."

Margaret looked at her, worried that her mother was delirious.

"All right, I believe you. And look, I've brought you a piece of candied ginger. The ginger is good for you."

"I may eat the ginger instead of the Holy Ghost." She took a bite, choking a little. "So good."

Margaret opened her wooden box, pulling from it the leather pouch. Untying its leather strings, she removed her Gospel-book.

"Where did you get that, Margaret? It's beautiful. Whose is it?"

"It's my very own. Abbot Máté and the nuns surprised me with it before we left home."

She showed her mother the gold lettering adorning the first page of each gospel and the portraits of the authors. Agatha ran her finger over the gold, impressed.

"A gift like this for a little girl? They must see how special you are, Margaret, like a pearl set in the center of a crown, dignified, singular, glowing from the layers within, yet formed around a grain of sand that irritates those who don't understand you."

"I'm not at all special, so there's nothing to understand. I'm dreary, haughty, and faithless."

Agatha smiled weakly, but Margaret was serious. She pressed the issue, to Agatha's surprise.

"Did I ever play as a child, mother?"

"Well, it always looked like a conscious effort, but play isn't of use as an adult, anyway, especially to a queen. You're going to be an adult much longer than you'll be a child. You could try to smile more often, though."

"I've tried smiling just to smile, but it's hard to remember. What does one smile about?"

"About the vagaries of life, which spurred on by Satan, play cruel jokes on you, but if you smile in spite of them at least the Devil doesn't win." She winked at Margaret. "Besides it makes untrustworthy people worry that they've been found out, which is useful when you need them to be off balance. Believe me, you'll have much to smile about when you see King Andrew's white castle, Székesfehérvár. It's magnificent. On the water. I must warn you, though, you'll see many pretty young women roaming about. They're untrustworthy, and beneath you. And often, beneath the king as well."

"Oh, mother, are you questioning the sanctity of his marriage?"

"There's a lack of chasteness everywhere, Margaret, even among our priests, which is why Pope Benedict VIII restricted the children of priests from inheriting property, hoping they'd stop having children."

Margaret sighed.

"He did? Now I have to worry about our priests' sanctity? First the abbot tells me there's only one way to love Ludmila, which I don't understand, and yet you say our priests defile love? I'm confused, Mother."

"Don't give it another thought. You came to read to me, didn't you?"

"Which gospel would you like to hear?"

"The Book of Luke. I like the way he writes. He's poetic."

Margaret read well and her voice soothed Agatha. Margaret watched her mother's breathing slow down before concluding she was asleep. She paused for a minute to study Agatha's face, then read on, too fascinated to stop at Luke. The sheer beauty of touching the Gospel-book's gold inscriptions and illuminations transported her. She loved the stories of Jesus. They made her feel as though He walked beside her, understanding what she felt, and suffering what she suffered. She was more confident than ever that He loved her, despite her dreariness and weaknesses.

Agatha opened one eye. She patted her daughter's hand and mumbled what sounded like a random comment. "Always remember why we named you Margaret," she said, before falling back asleep.

Margaret knew what she meant. Margaret of Antioch had been born in Syria seven hundred years earlier, with a pagan priest for a father and a mother who died shortly after giving birth to her. It was Margaret's nursemaid who made her a Christian. At fifteen, Margaret had been arrested and tortured before dying for her faith. Edward had first heard of the saint at Yaroslav's Eastern Orthodox court, where she was called Marina of Antioch. But the Western Church called her Margaret, and so Edward had chosen the Roman version for his firstborn. Margaret knelt on the floor to pray.

"Dear Margaret of Antioch," she whispered, "as one Margaret to another, lend me your strength and your faith. You sat in prison, not knowing what would happen, and I now kneel, not knowing what lies ahead for me. Please pray that I find peace. And more important, pray that I smile more often. Amen."

Margaret kissed her mother on the forehead and rejoined the feast, walking into the room with a frozen smile on her face, practicing her new skill.

She was stunned at the way people nodded and smiled back. How odd, thought Margaret. They've no idea that my smile is a mask, yet they presume my joy. Maybe this was a gift from Jesus, she wondered, although she'd never heard anything about Him smiling.

She still wore her practice smile when she finally found Ludmila eating alone in a corner.

"Are you enjoying your dinner, Ludmila?" Margaret beamed.

"What's wrong, Margaret?"

"Whatever do you mean?"

"I hardly recognize you. Doesn't that forced smile make your face hurt?"

Margaret relaxed her facial muscles. The charade was over.

"Yes, my cheeks are frozen. But no one else in the room noticed that it wasn't a real smile. They smiled back and looked happier than before they saw me. Does that always happen?"

"Usually. It's a skill I use sometimes, but I smile naturally, anyway, as part of my nature."

"It's not part of my nature. What am I supposed to do?"

"I think you're wonderful just as God made you. When you're happy, your eyes do the smiling. We're not to question why we're made short or tall, thin or fat. That's what Mother Anna Mária taught me when I cried because I'm not beautiful. 'Just trust Him,' she said."

"She's a gentle abbess."

"She's gentler than Abbot Máté, for certain, even if she's just as strict. But she's fair and she gives you more than one chance, because she says that's what the Lord does. The sinner always gets another chance. The abbot prefers to correct mistakes with whippings."

"Has he ever whipped you?"

"Twice. Now I do whatever he says. I suppose whippings work."

"Etel has slapped my hand a few times and Cristina was whipped a little, when she refused to do her lessons. But Etel has never raised a hand to Edgar."

"And she won't. We all know he's her favorite."

"He is very cute, so I can't blame her. And he's lots of fun, isn't he?"

"What's cute now, won't be cute two years from now. Benedict of Nursia says that youth who are at fault must receive just punishment."

"What kind of just punishment?"

"If the mistakes continue, he says the youth should be forced to fast or to be flogged."

"Father told me he was whipped as a boy. He says it made him a better man."

"Benedict of Nursia declares that, to do good works, we must first understand that evil comes from us and all good from the Lord; and we must desire Him above all else and fear hell."

"I definitely am afraid of hell! I pray for myself and everyone I know."

Ludmila hugged Margaret.

"So then, don't worry about fake smiles. Your prayers are worth more."

CHAPTER NINETEEN:

Esztergom

POOR Agatha. The wagon's wheels pitched over every rock and slipped into every rut the next morning. Two spokes cracked in a back wheel and she suffered greatly as they replaced it. Even so, she kept refusing the medicine prepared the prior evening; but by afternoon, she was begging for it. Brother János personally carried the tightly-stopped vial to her wagon, holding it gingerly, for he knew full well what was inside: a mixture of bile, lettuce, vinegar, bryony root, opium, hemlock and stinking nightshade. He'd personally overseen the potion's boiling process at the monastery, watching carefully, knowing too well of Agatha's frail condition.

His instructions to her attendants were emphatic.

"This is to help her rest through the pain. We're not doing surgery, so there's no need to put her into a deep sleep, which would be dangerous in her condition anyway. I alone will administer the doses. Let everyone here take note that she's receiving her first dose as the sun shines directly overhead. Let her rest, and when it's time to awaken her, wipe her temples with vinegar and put a cloth soaked with fennel into her nostrils. That should sharpen her awareness. If there are no questions, please bring me the wine now."

A cup of the court's finest wine was produced, into which Jónas stirred a spoonful of the potion.

"Help her sit up."

Agatha feebly tried to refuse the medicine one more time.

"My dear," said the brother, "you are in agony and the day is not yet half over. This is a very small dose. I'll check on you in a little while. If you need more medicine, you'll have it. If this proves sufficient, you needn't take it again."

"Yes, just this once," Agatha reluctantly agreed.

She forced down the nasty-tasting liquid, swallowing repeatedly to keep from throwing it back up.

A minstrel arrived to play his harp for her. The music calmed her and before he finished his second song, she was sound asleep.

The cavalcade halted at the village outside Esztergom late in the afternoon.

Now Edward had an urgent need to awaken Agatha.

"Give me more vinegar. We need to get her alert as quickly as possible."

Agatha stirred.

"Edward."

He kissed her on the cheek.

"My dear, We've a situation. A storm is blowing in and it's substantial. If we don't enter the city today, I fear we'll have to parade in a downpour tomorrow morning. We actually may have to tie you to that horse, after all, dirty hair and all, right now. Are you capable of riding?"

Agatha fought through the fog in her brain.

"Dear Edward, I'm not hungry. You say we've already arrived in England?"

"Oh dear," said Brother Jónas, burying his face in his hands.

"Don't be silly, doctor," insisted Agatha. "My head is a perfectly thinking mind," she said, falling back to sleep.

Her ladies spent the next two hours frantically stripping off her "sick" clothes and wiping her entire body with rose water, desperate to mask five days' worth of sweat and vomiting. They worked frantically to comb her hair into a style that wouldn't look like a mistake. Margaret fed her sprigs of parsley to kill the smell of vomit on her breath, while Etel continuously waved a vial of vinegar under her nose to keep her awake.

When they'd done all they could, Edward and Jónas draped Agatha's arms over their shoulders and walked her outside. The cold air revived her a bit, but they still tied her to her horse for safety's sake, especially since a woman of her stature needed to ride side saddle, to show off her clothing. Somehow, Agatha mustered the strength to appear elegant, although Edward could only speculate if she knew where she was. The sun was falling toward the nearly black horizon with alarming speed, and a sharp wind was blowing toward town. They had to move, now. The parade was vital, for this first impression would shape how the citizens of Hungary's capital received them.

By the time the procession was properly lined up, Esztergom already lay beneath oppressive rolls of wooly clouds, hanging in the sky.

"Those storm clouds are so low, we may have to push them back up a bit, just for some head room," said Edward, sniffing the moisture and praying the rain would hold off long enough for them to get through town and arrive dry at the royal castle.

The parade they'd made through Mecseknádasd paled in comparison to the one that was about to enter Esztergom, although they hurried it as fast as they could to beat the storm. Edward ordered that the horses be trotted down the street. But leading off the parade was a contingent of minstrels singing the praises of Edward and his family, knowing their voices would lure a crowd into the streets.

Behind the minstrels came the household workers and servants, displaying elements of their work: a kettle here, a flask of wine there, a hammer, sheep shearers, and wood-working tools.

They were followed by bleating goats and a flock of sheep. Behind the common livestock came the household's vehicles: more than one hundred gaily adorned wagons, carts and chariots. The clergy, nobles and their wives were next, the women waving sweetly to the spectators, who by now cheered their arrival. Included in this group were Nyék and Ludmila, riding side-by-side, Ludmila, chatting in awe over this large city, and Nyék, cynically observing the locals, who were willing to wait for an hour for the grand finale of the parade, which would be the royal family.

Edward's magnificent stable of horses drew cries of approval, as did his fine hunting dogs, and the endless crates of hooded falcons with their handlers. Finally came the royal family, the children first: Cristina and Edgar riding with the guards, the two youngsters waving and shouting hello, charming them all, and Margaret, looking several years older than she was, riding her horse gracefully, regal in her composure. The crowd murmured over her beauty.

At long last, Edward and Agatha came into view. The handsome couple riding on their pure white mounts was a glorious sight. The citizens, worried about King Andrew, were relieved to see his friend arrive. They prayed that this visit would spur on the king's recovery. Their cheers of joy fell sweet as rose petals on Edward and Agatha's ears.

The couple stopped in front of the royal residence just as fat raindrops were beginning to drop from the sky. King Andrew was not there to greet them, which was worrisome, but the rest of his court had lined up, smiling and eager to embrace the royal family.

Inside, the embassy's elites were greeted with a crackling fire. Agatha, Etel and the children gathered round it, turning their palms toward its warmth. Margaret's hands trembled a bit, as she took in the grandeur of the king's palace. She'd always thought Castle Réka was splendid, but this palace was beyond her imagining. Everything was bigger and more beautiful, made of expensive material, and it buzzed with many more people. Her mother was right. She noticed right away how many lovely young women walked the halls.

"Please take me to Andrew right now," were the first words out of Edward's mouth. The rest of the family would wait here and enjoy the food the servants were setting on a table. Agatha sank wearily into a chair.

Edward entered the king's chamber, catching his breath at his friend's weakened state. This frail man lying under the covers with the far-away look in his eyes was not the hearty sovereign Edward knew, but he couldn't let Andrew see his concern.

A moment later, Edward had to catch his breath again, for another sight shocked him even more: Bishop Ealdred stood at the head of Andrew's bed. Two thoughts flew through Edward's mind. Either the bishop was crafting a benevolent image by stopping to bless Andrew on his way to the Holy Land, or, more likely, he'd decided he wanted to influence the choice of Andrew's successor.

Pushing politics out of his mind for now, he ignored Ealdred and grasped Andrew's hand.

"My king, my friend, András. You are recovering?"

Andrew answered slowly; his words slurred.

"I can talk, somewhat."

"That's good news. We have much to talk about. There are important issues, but there is also friendship. With your permission, I will stay at the palace until you are satisfactorily recovered."

Andrew's smile was crooked.

"Then I assume you're not in a hurry to get to England."

"Not enough of one to abandon you. Tonight, your doctors will meet with me to explain your treatment. Perhaps you and I will talk tomorrow morning?"

"Unless I decide to go hunting," Andrew slurred.

"Your humor is intact. It's a good sign. I'll see you tomorrow."

He nodded curtly toward Ealdred.

"Your Excellency. Perhaps you and I will talk tomorrow, too."

The bishop barely looked up before speaking.

"You must be tired. Rest well."

By the time Edward joined his family for some repast, Agatha was already asleep.

"Father," Margaret asked, "how is the king?"

"I'd say he's improving, but I'll feel better after I meet with his physicians tonight."

He caught Nyék out of the corner of his eye, walking past the door.

"Nyék! Come in here."

The tutor was thrilled to be noticed. He hurried in.

"Yes, Sire?"

"I see you are carrying the medical volumes. Good. Bring them with you when we meet with the king's physicians tonight."

"Of course. I've been studying Isidore and Galen since you entrusted the books to me. I'm prepared to discuss everything with the doctors."

"No, you will wait until I bring you into the conversation."

Nyék cringed. Again, he'd managed to say the wrong thing.

"Yes, my liege. Of course. I would never insert myself ..."

"Thank you. Why don't you stay and eat with the family?"

Nyék was speechless with joy.

"Father," said Margaret, "may Ludmila sleep with me while we're staying here? When we leave Esztergom, she has to return to the abbey. I'm going to miss her so much."

"I don't see why not. Nyék, you and Ludmila seem to enjoy time in each other's company. Please go find her and bring her here. We'd like to have her join us for our meal."

Nyék bit his lip. That cursed lay sister, a simple girl whose only virtue was her strength out in the fields. Now he had to leave the inner circle to find and include her. He felt less special.

"My pleasure, Sire. I'll find her and bring her back with me as quickly as possible."

He just hoped there would still be hot food on the table.

After dinner, the physicians gave Edward a detailed accounting of Andrew's stroke, how it happened and his chances for a productive recovery. Edward and Nyék, who still had the medical books attached to his arm, left the meeting together.

"I'm feeling encouraged, Nyék."

"As am I, Sire."

"Andrew could continue to rule, even if his speech doesn't come all the way back. But the question of succession looms large."

"His son is very young. That's an obstacle."

"A bigger obstacle is the man who will be celebrating Mass tomorrow morning."

"The bishop? Why do you think he came here, when he said he wasn't going to?"

"He's an ambitious man. One might even suspect simony, given how many sees he holds and the multiple abbeys he administers. I'm not sure he's likable enough for multiple positions without some gold coins exchanging hands. But he does have the trust of my uncle, the Confessor. He's a shrewd politician."

"Whom do you think the bishop wants to see on the Hungarian throne?"

"I'm certain that Béla, Andrew's brother, is more to his liking than young Salomon. When we were all living at Yaroslav's court, I knew Béla, but we spent little time together because I neither liked nor trusted him. He's much less forthcoming than Andrew. Certainly, he feels he should have secured the crown over Andrew."

"What will you do?"

"First, I want to hear Andrew's wishes directly from his mouth. Then, I'll attempt to divine Ealdred's intentions. It's unfortunate that the bishop is here. I thought he'd removed himself from the situation to pilgrimage to Jerusalem. But if I'm going to rule England, I'm must be able to read the minds of ambitious men, and he's a challenge."

"Perhaps Rome will slap him down someday."

"Perhaps. Nyék, while you're studying Galen's medical volumes, find me his military treatises on Archimedes' weapons, particularly his weapons to destroy ships, you know, the mirrors and the arms to shake ships. I wish to refresh my memory before meeting with the bishop."

"Yes, Sire. It's my honor to assist you."

CHAPTER TWENTY:

Crisis

MARGARET and Ludmila lay snuggled in bed, arms around each other, whispering, so as not to wake Cristina and Edgar, who'd fallen long ago asleep. The girls were too excited for sleep.

"How long do you think your father will want to stay with King Andrew?"

"Not until the king is much better, I'm sure. That will probably take a long time, don't you think?"

"Don't I think? Don't I hope! This court is exciting. Why do you want to be a nun, Margaret, when you're part of something so important?"

"Because I want to go to heaven. And when I pray for others, I want my prayers to be pure enough to be heard by Jesus, so those I love can go to heaven, too. I have to be a nun to do that."

"I don't know why. I think you're already an angel."

"No, I'm not. Remember the horrible thing I said to you? I almost lost your friendship and I'll spend my life atoning for the sins of my mouth."

"You'll never lose me, at least not my heart. When someone truly loves you, they can make all kinds of mistakes and you'll forgive them without even noticing. I'll pray for you every day, for your health and for your return to Hungary."

"And I'll pray for you. And for my return to Hungary. And if I can't come back to Mecseknádasd, I'll bring you to wherever I am."

They whispered for another hour, until yawns interrupted their sentences, and their eyelashes became too heavy to open after blinking.

It was nearly dawn when they were awakened by screams.

Margaret sat upright; her eyes big.

"That's my mother! That's her screaming!"

"She must be in terrible pain."

Margaret was already getting dressed. She flew out the door before Ludmila could find where she'd kicked off her shoes.

The hallway in front of Agatha's bed chamber was crowded with people wringing their hands and crying.

The screams were horrifying. Margaret pushed through the crowd and had her hand on the door latch before one of King Andrew's guards stopped her.

"No, Miss. No one else is to enter. Not even you. Edward's orders."

"But I'm their eldest daughter!"

"I'm sorry, Milady. They're doing everything they can, and the room is overflowing, already."

"Is my father in there?"

"Yes, he was the first one here."

Margaret's knees buckled beneath her. She slid down the wall in a heap, sobbing, her face in her hands, with salty tears seeping between her fingers.

"Lord have mercy. Jesus have mercy. Mercy!"

She heard a doctor shouting a stream of orders inside the bed chamber. Bowls banged together. Water was being poured.

Someone called out, "More blankets!"

A woman said, "On this side! Someone, help me!"

Margaret nearly fainted to hear her father say, "Can't you stop the bleeding? How could you not know? Please, I cannot lose her!"

The screams seemed to go on forever, until suddenly, the room went silent. Had her mother just died, and here she sat outside the door? Margaret thought her heart would explode, not knowing if her mother were alive. She rushed the door, pounding on its thick wood, and ignoring the guards' entreaties.

"Father," she yelled at the top of her lungs. "Let me in! Please, let me in!"

"Just Margaret, no one else," she heard him say.

Edward was draped across Agatha's torso, sobbing. Her mother wasn't moving. Her face was ash white and there was blood everywhere: on the bed, the pillows and on the linens strewn across the floor. The doctor, wiping blood off his hands and arms, looked around unsuccessfully for a clean towel, unaware that his face was smeared with blood anyway.

"Take heart, little one," he said to Margaret.

"Is she ..."

Margaret couldn't say the word.

Edward held out his hand to her and shared the truth, his voice husky with emotion.

"Your mother was pregnant, but she didn't tell me because she knew I wouldn't have let her travel. It's all my fault. The doctors told me she shouldn't get pregnant again, that it was too dangerous for her; but she was hoping to produce another heir. It's my fault, all of it."

Margaret stood mutely, staring. Her mother's hand trailed off the edge of the bed, a soft finger pointing to something across the room, as though she could see someone she knew and wanted to introduce them; however, her eyes were fixed on the ceiling, clearly looking like she was waiting for someone coming to pick her up. Margaret was terrified that the angels were coming. She watched to see if a dove flew out of her mother, a sure sign that her soul was leaving, but she saw nothing.

"Is she ..."

"She's still alive, barely. She shouldn't have tried to carry this child. Her great strength has been undone by her even greater stubbornness."

"Why did she hide her condition when she could have drunk gin and juniper and ended it?"

"Because she deems it her sacred duty to produce heirs."

"She offered her life to fulfill her sacred duties."

"Don't encourage the Lord to take her, Margaret. She's still with us. I'm counting on that the stubborn streak to keep here. She's just lost so much blood and her insides are shredded." He placed his mouth to Agatha's ear, so only she could hear. "Think about riding with our falcons through the fresh morning air, my darling. Your horses are stamping about, waiting for your gentle touch and guidance. And I'll throw you the biggest feast you've ever had, with every decoration you choose and any food you want. Then in the middle of it, you and I will slip away and walk under the moon to talk and laugh. I can't plan without you. You know that, dear Agatha. Stay with me."

His voice choked.

"Margaret, find Etel and tell her your mother has suffered a grave miscarriage. Then the two of you can share the news with your brother and sister. We must keep up a good appearance at the king's court, especially since he's not well, either."

"Yes, father. And you know I'll be praying."

"Good girl. I'm trying to as well. It's just difficult."

"Then groan your prayers, Father. The angels will translate them into proper prayers and carry them to God's ears."

Outside the door, Margaret leaned against a wall, trying to gulp air. Fear squeezed the breath from her lungs. Once she was able to inhale, she headed straight to the king's chapel, to remind the Holy Mother of her promise to pray for her mother's recovery.

"I love you, Blessed Mother, and I know you heard me, but I will persist, because I have to. Your Son will listen to you and heal my mother. Don't forget, her name is Agatha. And I'm Margaret, leaving my heart with you, as a sacrifice, to give to your son, Jesus. I thank you with all my faith. Amen."

Then she went in search of Etel.

It was quiet around Agatha's bed. The women cleaned up in silence after the doctor left.

Edward spoke.

"May I see the child?"

"It hardly looks real," said one of the ladies in waiting.

"Please."

A nun brought over a bowl. Inside lay what looked like a tiny doll, smaller than his palm. Edward peered at the whiff of life and pushed away a surge of emotion. Its little legs were crossed, and its thumb was in its mouth.

"Can you identify the gender?"

"Oh, no, Sire. It was much too soon. The child is no more than three months *in utero*."

"Agatha endured so much; she must have believed it was a boy. I will hold my son."

The nun carefully placed the embryo into his cupped hands.

"I name him Edmund, after my father. Godspeed, Edmund."

He turned to a nun.

"Please see that he's baptized and buried in your church yard. A small grave for a small child, who might have been a great king."

He gently placed the embryo back into the bowl.

"Rest in peace, Edmund. Your mother wanted you so much, she was willing to die for you. In the name of the Father, the Son and the Holy Ghost."

Agatha stirred.

"Could you hear me, Agatha? Do you approve?"

She nodded; eyes closed.

"The Lord has taken our child, but I've faith that He's going to let me keep you. You will live, won't you, Agatha?"

She smiled and wiggled her fingers. With that she went back to sleep, utterly spent. It would be days before she could sit up in bed.

Edward left for his chambers, intent on taking some time to relax, to gather his thoughts and to manage the complicated situations in which he was ensconced. He fell asleep before he knew he was sleepy and snored until he was startled awake by a rapping at the door. It was Ealdred's right hand man, rudely interrupting his rest.

"Sire, Bishop Ealdred has summoned you for a meeting."

Although groggy, Edward was clear on one thing: He would not allow Ealdred to control the parameters of their meeting.

Without stirring, Edward said, "Please assure the good bishop that I will arrange for our meeting tomorrow. I appreciate learning of his availability."

The bishop's messenger was stunned to be turned away, but he stammered, "Yes, of course. I will inform the bishop of your prompt response. I'm sure he'll be ... pleased to await a later meeting."

"The good bishop wouldn't kill the messenger, now would he?"

"Oh, no, Sire!" He laughed weakly, worry pulling the skin around his eyebrows.

Edward smiled, relaxed by establishing the boundaries of this cockfight. The empowerment was freeing. He slept another hour before arising.

The first thing he did was to kneel before the chamber's *triptych* set into the wall in a niche to pray for the repose of the soul of his father, Edmund Ironside, and his wife's recovery from the miscarriage, and for the soul of his unborn son.

Margaret broke the news about the miscarriage as gently as possible to the two younger children.

"Mother is very tired, but you know her, she's so strong she'll be chasing you down the hall, Edgar, sooner than you want!"

Etel interjected, "Yes, but until she's ready for that, you must let her take as much rest as she needs, first. Are we clear on that, Lord Goose?"

"Yes, Nanny." He was scared. "But now I'm really sorry we left home."

CHAPTER TWENTY-ONE:

Political Gamesmanship

EDWARD looked impassively at Ealdred when the bishop entered his personal chamber room. Edward's eyes were unblinking, his breathing steady, and his mind uncluttered, like a master chess player waiting to begin his game. But he was in no hurry to make the first move.

"Your Excellency. Please, sit."

The bishop smiled confidently but squirmed a bit when a bland-faced Edward said nothing more. He finally felt compelled to start the conversation.

"You were surprised to see me here in Ezstergom, I imagine."

Edward nodded, but said nothing. He didn't care what had made the bishop change his mind, although he was certain the reasons involved an agenda to benefit himself.

"The King of Hungary is very ill. He required anointing before I continue onto Jerusalem."

Edward nodded slightly and quietly raised an eyebrow.

"The Lord does speak to me and thus guides me exquisitely along the path of my pastoral duties."

"Admirable."

"I'm a simple priest."

"Simple is a word that slides right off of you."

Ealdred bristled.

"I'm proud to serve our king in all capacities, but fundamentally, I have a pastoral soul."

"And apparently a forgiving one, given your distaste for King Andrew and your affection for his brother, Béla."

There it was, shot across the bow - and it was only Edward's first move.

Bishop Ealdred was caught off guard by the directness of the accusation. But Edward was correct; if Andrew died, Ealdred would support the Polish-bred brother, rather than the king's young son. And he chose not to deny it.

"Andrew has crossed swords with me in a way Béla has not."

"But a simple priest, or even a simple bishop with a pastoral soul, has the ear of God, yes?"

"Yes. He also has the ear of your half-uncle, who sits on the throne of England."

"And who commanded you to bring me to his side as his successor."

Bishop Ealdred narrowed his eyes at Edward's last statement. Edward briefly mused over whom Ealdred might prefer on the throne of England, instead of him, but he knew he wasn't yet familiar enough with the country's political powers to speculate. Ealdred knew that as well.

More silence.

Edward relaxed and smiled, helping himself to a pear from the fruit bowl, sinking his teeth into it - a big bite, calculated to make juice run down his arm. It was page torn from Andrew's book, to show the bishop he wasn't afraid of him, by unsettling his brittle personality. A fastidious man, Ealdred was repulsed watching the juice seep into Edward's sleeve. Ironically, the bishop's thin skin, which made him irritable, also aided his ability to read a situation. It was clear to him that Edward had sniffed out his plan to pressure the weakened Andrew into naming his brother Béla as successor.

Edward grabbed another pear and tossed it to Ealdred, who bobbled it before catching it.

"You have deft reactions, Your Excellency."

"So do you," replied an flustered Bishop Ealdred. He set the pear on the table like a chess piece on a board, his face red with anger, and he barely paused before mounting his counter-offensive. It was a thinly-veiled threat.

"I'm sure you realize that being called to a throne and the path to actually sitting upon that throne is more treacherous than the journey you're taking from Hungary to England."

Edward let the arrow to fly right past him. He took another casual bite of pear.

The bishop continued, trying again to ignore him.

"Andrew invited his brother Béla back to Hungary to administer one-third of the country in preparation for turning the throne over to him. I've read the letter so many times, I can quote it. '… I ask you, most beloved brother, that you come to me without delay, so that we may be companions in joy and share in the good things of kingdom, rejoicing in each other's presence. For I have neither heir nor brother I love, except you. You shall be my successor in the kingdom.' All three brothers were bastards of Vasul and his concubine, anyway."

"A trivial situation, as well you know, and since that letter our good King András has had a son, Salomon, his legitimate heir."

"Who is five years old."

"As is my son, Edgar. I'm curious, Your Excellency, would you deprive my son, the last heir of the House of Wessex, and an Anglo-Saxon, of his birthright to the throne of England if I declared him my successor?"

His own words caused pangs of regret to wash over Edward. He thought about Agatha's heroic efforts to provide him with another heir. He prayed again that she would survive the damage this last pregnancy had done to her body. Ealdred saw his face contort and noted the emotion.

"How is Agatha? She is a noble woman."

"With the strength of the Lord and the care of the king's court, I'm encouraged she will survive."

Bishop Ealdred's face softened, not from sympathy, for his heart had little concern for women, but because he knew that, regardless of whatever he agreed to today, he would be able to change the situation later on. He had confidence in the force of his ego. He shrugged.

"Why not? Let us coronate Andrew's young suckling. I don't care."

Edward knew he was being played, but he'd broker the best deal he could and hope that history would see it through. He made his demand.

"Thank you, Your Excellency; however, first Béla must choose the sword of the duchy and foreswear the crown before you leave Hungary."

"A paralyzed king like Andrew wears a slippery crown. I'm doubtful how much power he holds, but fine, we will crown the lad and solidify his marriage with the Holy Roman Empire's Princess Judith. Either way, I'll stay in Hungary no longer. The Holy Land awaits me, and I'll waste no more time on this matter."

"What gift are you bringing to Jerusalem?"

"A gold chalice for the empty tomb of our Risen King."

"You've a penchant for desiring lofty places."

Ealdred was caught off-guard. Edward had slipped in a particularly well-timed barb. It was well known that the bishop had a way of collecting bishoprics, acquiring power and wealth in the process. His close relationship with Edward the Confessor allowed for such things to be swept under the rug, but if Edward Aetheling replaced Edward the Confessor on the throne – well, Ealdred would have to finesse his ambitions more carefully. He had just been served notice.

Fine, he thought. He'd accrue all the stature he could in the meantime. Edward was smart, but he was a rank novice in English politics. The bishop not only knew where the bodies were buried, but where others soon would be.

For his part, Edward knew he'd done all he could hope to for now. Ealdred would be out of the picture while in Jerusalem, buying him time to personally forge foreign relationships without the bishop's influence.

He waited until the bishop reached the door to interrupt his exit.

"Mm, Ealdred. I require another moment of your time. I would appreciate your expert opinion on a military matter."

"Really."

"Yes. I've been studying Galen's writings on the brilliant Archimedes' contributions to naval warfare. You are familiar, I assume?"

Ealdred cocked his head.

"Of course, I'm familiar."

"If you were a citizen of Syracuse as Archimedes was, and under siege by Roman ships, which of his military inventions would you select to employ as your main defense?"

Ealdred smirked. This discussion wasn't about effective weaponry. Selecting one method over the other exposed a moral position about his attitude toward warfare. But he was delighted to play the game and make his beliefs clear.

"Livy writes about Archimedes' war machines as well, and there are discrepancies between his accounts and Galen's, of which I'm sure you're aware. Personally, my choice would be the Archimedes Claw."

"Do you refer to beams swinging from the walls and dropping weights to sink the ships, or the Claw, grabbing a ship at the bow, lifting it from the water and shaking men from the ship?"

"The Claw itself. Whether the men fall into the sea or are dashed onto the rocks, the effect is the same."

"Why not use his stone throwers?"

"Not forceful enough."

"Then why not his parabola of bronze shields concentrating sunlight until the Roman ships burst into flames?"

"Artistic, but much too slow. And they might not work at all. Wars are not meant to be beautiful. They are meant to be won."

"No. The Claw, then, of course. Because …?"

"It creates the greatest terror for those in the ship and those in the ships around it."

"Fear is war's most effective weapon, without question."

"And you, Edward? Which is your preference?"

"I concur with you in the Claw's effectiveness, but I find the mirrors more dramatic."

Well, thought the bishop, therein lies the difference between a warrior and a naïve king.

Edward Aetheling read his thoughts and let them hang silently in the room. He would end this conversation with unresponsiveness. He meant to keep Ealdred off balance as much as he possibly could, intending to keep him in the dark, without a reaction.

Ultimately, the meeting ended in a stalemate. Volleys had purposely been tossed wide of their marks. Neither man had backed down but neither had one bested the other. Although the end result was unsatisfying for both, it was the most practical outcome for now. Each man would continue to stall and position themselves, until it was time for action.

CHAPTER TWENTY-TWO:

King Andrew's Nosegays

NURSE Etel had warned Margaret to "stay away from those faded, putrid nosegays," but Margaret found the flouncing lovelies filling the halls of King Andrew's court amusing, in spite of her better instincts. She coveted their bright, feminine clothing, and longed to overhear the stories they whispered to one another; each one more amusing than the last, judging from their rising squeals. She'd never been around girls like them. She could tell they were immodest and vain, but they fascinated her. And they always smiled and laughed. She was intrigued.

These "nosegays" were equally intrigued by this rural guest from the south. Birds of prey, they homed in on Margaret's beauty; and even though her figure had barely begun to sprout; and although her royal status placed her above them, they still relished speculating wickedly about her sexual potential. It was their *raison d'etre,* and their world, after all.

"You're like me, young," giggled one about Margaret's age. "The court is waiting for the right time when I will 'bloom' for King Andrew. What a night that will be."

Standing behind her was an experienced, voluptuous girl of about nineteen, who snorted knowingly.

"Bloom? Your private parts are so tightly stitched, the king's ladies-in-waiting will have to snip you open one petal at a time before you can 'bloom.' I'll enjoy hearing you scream in pain all the way from the stables."

The young girl retorted.

"Of course, you'll be in the stables: your worn-out petals are so loose on the stem that it takes a stallion for you to notice you've been invaded."

"Why, you thin-lipped, withering rosebud. King András is a stallion, and a warrior I've pleased until my jewelry box is filled with stones of every color. Even in his current state, whom do you suppose he has asked for tonight?"

"You'd better hope those stones will keep you warm at night. At your age, you're nearly finished, and there's not a nobleman who will want to marry you. A feeble-minded peasant, perhaps. An old, ugly, poor, feeble-minded peasant."

The other girls tittered.

"I don't need to marry. The king will take care of me."

"One more stroke and we'll have a new king. Then who will you spend your nights with? Oh, but you don't care, do you?"

Margaret wasn't following the conversation particularly well but wanted to participate.

"So, our king enjoys your company? How lovely. Will you go riding tonight? Or perhaps play chess? It's another wonderful way to spend a night."

The girls were momentarily silent, before bursting into raucous laughter.

Margaret felt bewildered and humiliated. The nineteen-year-old took pity on her, and remembering her own long-lost virginity, placed a protective arm around her.

"It's okay, little bird. You're probably right. The king and I will likely do a little bit of horseback riding tonight."

The other girls snickered. The older girl whispered into Margaret's ear.

"Look, with any luck the king who first takes you will be your husband. You've a good chance at that in a year or so, especially with your father sitting on a throne. Turn your backbone into iron, though, to fend off the likes of me. Unless you don't care about who keeps your husband warm. Queen Anastasia doesn't care. It gives her a night off. He wears her out."

"Do you really want to be a baby maker for a king?" asked the youngest of the girls. "A queen pushing out heir after heir, when they rarely use the line of succession anyway?"

"How does it matter what she wants?"

"My mother died giving birth," said another.

"So did mine," said another. "The baby right after me. They both died. She was twenty."

"You just have to know what to drink to kill the baby," said the nineteen-year-old casually.

Margaret thought of her mother's miscarriage and her fragile state of health, and her heart froze. Interest in this conversation flew away like a crow frightened away from carrion.

Luckily for Margaret, Ludmila appeared. She was as innocent as Margaret, but as an orphaned peasant rescued by the monastery, she was constant prey for men who thought she might be looking for fun, and she sized up Margaret's predicament.

"Leave the princess alone!"

She took Margaret gently by the arm.

"Come, sweet one. Let's go for a walk."

"I want to visit my mother. Please, Ludmila, right now."

Etel had suspected the situation and came flying around the corner.

"Shoo, you rotted pieces of fruit! You demean the House of Wessex with your wickedness. Off to confession with you, if you can find a priest less corrupt than you."

The girls giggled and strolled down the hall, arm in arm, seemingly unconcerned, although that night several stayed awake, soberly fearing that their souls would burn in hell when they died, and more than one wiped away a troubled tear.

Etel and Ludmila steered Margaret directly to Agatha's room, where her ladies-in-waiting were caring for her. She was starting to get color back in her face and optimism was growing that not only would the queen survive, but that the royal party might soon again be traversing *en route* to England.

"Margaret was just accosted by King Andrew's girls. I fear she's in shock."

Agatha sighed.

"The necessary evils of most courts. I suppose it's time she learned. Everyone out of the room, please. Margaret, come sit on the edge of my bed."

"You look better today, Mother."

"And you look like you've seen an evil spirit. Were the girls mean to you?"

"No. Yes. I'm not sure. I couldn't follow what they were talking about, but at first, they thought I did. Then they laughed at me."

"That's because you are a pearl in a sea of codfish. You couldn't be like them no matter how hard you tried, nor do you want to be. They've sold their souls to the worldly needs of men and their rewards are worldly. You've set your heart on the rewards of God's kingdom. But forgive them, don't dislike them. The Church winks at brothels, and even clergy take advantage of cheap sex. It's the way of the world."

"Those girls have sex with King Andrew? That's what 'blooming' is?"

"Is that what they're calling it? I hadn't heard that one. Yes, they have sex with him."

"They said Queen Anastasia doesn't care, that it gives her 'a night off.' You know her. Is it true that she doesn't care? Aren't women supposed to be chaste? And aren't men not to covet another man's ox, or his wife?"

Agatha laughed.

"In that order?"

The truth was about to hit Margaret, as Agatha knew it would. She studied Margaret's face as she thought the question and then scrounged for the courage to ask it.

"Mother," she said, slowly forming the words. "What about Father? I've never seen girls like these at Castle Réka. Does he …?"

"First of all, your father and I respect each other. He would never embarrass me by openly having girls like that at court. Do I think he dallies? Yes, perhaps he does. But royal heirs are the most important thing to emanate from a royal marriage and we've tried diligently to produce them, so I don't think he has much time for other women. But Margaret, I lost a child before you and now I've lost another one. If I get pregnant again, the doctors assure me both the child and I will die. I'm not a young woman and your father is a vibrant man. Will I condemn him if he turns to other women, whether for procreation or recreation? My position in his life is secure and our family is consecrated to God. I assure you; he'd rather talk to me than to any of those young dimwits. When you are married to a king, I think you'll understand. Your father and I will do our best to find you a good man, Margaret, but you must recognize that being a queen is a political position."

Margaret was alarmed.

"Mother, you know that I'm going to be a nun. It's all I've ever wanted!"

"Margaret, this is difficult for you to hear, I know, but your destiny lies in your bloodline, especially now. If the Confessor hadn't called for your father, you might have been able to be a nun, but things have changed. There will be alliances to be made, but we'll make them carefully, I promise you. And queens pray quite as much as nuns do, for there's always much to pray about. You can do great good as a queen."

Margaret was distraught. She didn't care anymore about young girls having sex. She was engulfed in despair. Her life was ruined, and she was still powerless to fix it.

CHAPTER TWENTY-THREE:

Journeying On

ISHOP Ealdred celebrated morning Mass, then evaporated from court. He'd coronated young Salomon the previous evening, with no intention of letting him ever wear the crown, of course. But he was finally free of Esztergom and King Andrew. Ahead of him lay Jerusalem, and he was eager to claim the badge of a Holy Land pilgrim, for it would lend him an aura of spirituality, as it did any pilgrim who'd been there. Even better, he would be the first English bishop to make the journey. Yes, he would carry the humble pilgrim's staff, even if he didn't walk a step; sleep by holy tombs and leave behind gifts for the land where Jesus trod and healed and died and rose again; but he also planned to return to England with many relics destined for silver and gold and enameled reliquaries - impressive gifts for the wealthy and full of healing power; as well as special adornment for his personal landholdings and bishoprics. Every altar required a relic, and he'd make certain that his were from dramatically martyred saints, with power stored in their body parts or clothing or objects that had touched them. His status would be elevated, in both the Eastern and the Western Church. He smiled, withdrawing his sword from his scabbard to point east, his standard bearer holding high his banner, leading him forward, as his most dedicated soldiers encircled him on horseback. Let no robber think he could assail Bishop Ealdred on this journey. He was under the guard of Saint Michael, warrior to warrior. He was certain of that. Yes, he smiled. Yes.

No one missed Ealdred, for something more momentous happened later that day: Agatha left her bed chambers, bathed, dressed and smiling. Edward, Margaret, Cristina, Edgar and the entire household lined up to welcome her back to the land of the healthy. The family had survived a major crisis and their journey toward England could now continue.

It seemed that all of Esztergom rejoiced with them. King Andrew and Queen Anastasia embraced the family and gave presents to each member. Nearly everyone in Esztergom thronged the streets to wish them Godspeed. Even King Andrew's playthings, his young nosegays, stood together to wave goodbye to Margaret. Her beauty and sweetness had touched them, and they were genuinely sorry to see her go.

But the hardest goodbye had been that between Margaret and Ludmila. The seminal moment had occurred right after Mass. It was time for Ludmila to return to life at Pécsvárad Abbey, while Margaret, who had decided to no longer think of her childhood at Castle Réka, would only look forward from now on. A gulf was developing between them.

Still, it was a poignant goodbye, one too meaningful for tears. Margaret's hands remained steady, her chin, set. Ludmila studied Margaret's face, imprinting Margaret's stark blue eyes on her memory, so that whenever she looked at the Hungarian sky, she'd see her friend. But that waif who prayed by the stream no longer lived in those eyes. Margaret was more complex now.

Margaret gently took Ludmila's hands into her own.

"I'm so grateful for our time together here. I will pray for you every morning at Mass, Ludmila."

"As I will for you, dear Margaret."

"Please thank Abbess Anna Mária and the other nuns for the Gospel-book. It will never leave my side."

"I'll tell them, and we will eagerly await word from England. Your father's rule will bless the country of England."

"By the grace of our Lord, Jesus, yes, it will."

"And you will be a great queen one day."

Margaret grew even more serious, while remaining uncharacteristically unsentimental.

"Ludmila, whatever lies ahead for me, I vow that one day, you and I will be reunited. I'll bring you to join my household, wherever it may be. Should that be in my power, and within God's will, it will be done."

Margaret's face momentarily softened, as a tiny smile played with the corner of her mouth.

"Of course, if it's God's will for me to take the veil instead, be it in Hungary or England, I'll gladly relinquish worldly power and live as Christ's bride. Perhaps the Confessor, pious king that he is, will hear my heart's desire and grant it to me."

"Then may I pray for that, Margaret?"

"No, my will is no longer of consequence until I receive a clear sign from the Lord. Until then, I have no will of my own."

"Then how shall I pray for you?"

"Always with the *Pater Noster*, Ludmila, the words our Lord gave us. And the Psalms. Pray for my humility, for as I pray, I may be able carry others with me to heaven, if I am worthy, but only if I'm worthy. I don't think I can do it without your prayers, dear Ludmila, you who knows me better than anyone."

"I'll see you in the geese flying overhead, dropping surprise feathers of grace on your head, and I'll watch for the *albus* hart. How shall you pray my soul out of purgatory, Margaret? I think I'm hopeless."

"My first prayer will always be that your stomach feels full, lest you raid the *cellarium* too often for extra food."

Ludmila laughed, but Margaret was serious.

"Your heart is pure, so I won't call it stealing, but since it's done in secret, you still must confess your sin. Then I will pray for your spiritual education, lest Satan, with his beauty, deceive and tempt you. And finally, I pray that you perform acts of charity, for Ludmila, I cannot describe the joy I felt washing the old peasant woman's feet, and I wish that joy for you."

"I will miss you."

"Our hearts remain intertwined until we meet again."

Ludmila was about to head to her pack horse. She was joining a small group of traders journeying south down the Danube River to bring supplies to Pécsvárad Abbey. She shouted after the men to please wait one more moment for her to say farewell to her friend.

"Hurry up!" shouted the guide.

The two girls looked at each other. There was nothing more to say for now. Margaret spoke only one more sentence to Ludmila.

"I'm not going to watch you leave, my dear friend, for I'm confident that this is not really goodbye."

The guide called out to Ludmila.

"We're leaving without you if you don't come now."

Ludmila said, "I'm coming! Please, one more moment."

Ludmila turned back to wish her friend well, one last time.

But Margaret was already walking away, slipping behind the thick wall of the outer castle, just out of sight, closing her eyes to imagine Ludmila's departure. She was afraid to break her vow not to watch, lest it destroy the promise of a future reunion.

Margaret knew now the she couldn't control what was coming next in her life. She had no choice but to trust the Lord, yet, with her mother nearly restored to health, and her own faith re-emerging from a dark period, she realized that an unknown destiny might simply be grace as yet unmanifested. That was a feeling she'd had when she prayed by her stream: the feeling that she was never alone, that she could trust Him to take care of her. It was heady stuff for an eleven-year-old. For now, she only knew and accepted that ahead lay the Holy Roman Empire, and that the comforts of Lent and Easter, ancient holy days that solidified the rhythm of their lives, were upcoming.

Beyond that, lay England, a complete unknown.

As it turned out, Margaret was enthralled by traversing north on the fast-flowing Danube. She and her family enjoyed traveling on a shallow draught Mora, a colorful boat with the Scandinavian overtones that appealed to Edward. It was a beautiful mode of transportation and the swift water made the distances fly by, especially in comparison to the horrible Roman roads they'd bumped along to reach Esztergom. The river was an exciting place – such a world as she'd never seen – in truth, the world was bigger than she could have imagined! Each city presented the opportunity for another parade through a town, and Father had let her ride alongside him through the bustling trading city of Vienna. It was a glorious experience. Margaret stood up in her saddle to better see the remains of the ancient Roman military camp of Vindoboda, which made Edward chuckle.

"Yes, little one, the Romans were here a very long time ago, but remember, the Magyars were still here until about one hundred years ago, when they were defeated in battle. Which is more impressive to you?"

"The Magyars! Ut! Ut!"

"So, you haven't completely forgotten Hungary yet?"

"Oh, never, Father. I'm just not going to attend a Requiem Mass for it every day. There's too much else I haven't seen yet. Will you visit the Bishop of Vienna?"

"I just found out they don't have one, as important as the city is to the Holy Roman Empire. Perhaps as King of England, I can help fix that."

"So, that's why we didn't stop?"

"Yes, but don't feel like you've missed anything. Wait until we go around that bend up ahead. I've heard a lot about a beautiful gorge not too far past there, and then comes Weltenberg Abbey, where we'll stay tonight. They're famous for their beer, Margaret. Let's enjoy it."

When the gorge appeared, Margaret craned her neck in astonishment to see the tops of its magnificent cliffs plunging straight down into the water. Edward halted the cavalcade and encouraged the children to clamor through some of its caves before having the local guides lead the party to the Abbey.

Everyone agreed that Weltenberg was one of their favorite stops on the journey, most likely influenced by the amount of beer that flowed. It was nearly a week of partying before anyone felt like moving on.

Eventually, the days drifted by like the scenery did along the riverbanks. Sometimes Margaret wasn't sure where they were, nor did she really care. It was pretty and new.

And while the remaining English contingent seemed eager to cross the waterway to England, the Hungarians were savoring the hospitality and recognition they received at each of the ancient Roman cities they visited, gaining confidence in their eventual reception in England with each passing day.

Agatha moved within her new sphere of influence quietly, but astutely, never drawing attention away from her husband. Margaret tried to absorb her attitude, spending time with her father whenever it was possible, which wasn't often, but trying to enjoy the journey without requiring much attention from either parent. She studied her English and French lessons and indulged herself in the prayer time her soul craved, whenever possible.

Her siblings, though, had been cut from a different cloth. Cristina was still madly in love with Pál, flirting relentlessly and hoping they'd never reach England, while young Edgar pretended that every day brought him closer to sitting on the throne of England. While his studies would always overtax his focus, Edgar endlessly trained in hand-to-hand combat – a good little soldier-to-be, with more enthusiasm than talent.

They were in Regensburg on Ash Wednesday, the first day of Lent.

"Do you feel Charlemagne's spirit, Margaret?"

"Yes! The Holy Roman Empire is so big. And so many people in Regensburg! I think they've all come to today's Lenten service."

Indeed, the cathedral was packed. Edward's party alone nearly filled its edifice. Before distributing ashes to the faithful, the local bishop recalled a homily given about fifty years earlier by a popular Anglo-Saxon priest, Aelfric, Abbot of Eynsham.

"And after reminding his flock," said the bishop, "that men repented of their sins by adorning their bodies with ashes and sackcloth in both the Old Law and the New Law, Abbot Aelfric said to his faithful, 'Now let us do this little at the beginning of our Lent that we strew ashes upon our heads to signify that we ought to repent of our sins during the Lenten fast.' Heed Aelfric, I beg you, and I ask this little of you today, for only with this little can we begin to atone for the sins that lie rotting in our hearts."

Margaret felt her heart burning with shame as she conjured up all the potential sins she could have or could eventually commit to offend God. Her childish imagination went wild in an effort to confront what she considered her sinful side. Better to think of her sins before she committed them, she decided. As she struggled to fabricate a list in her mind, the adults around her wept less repentant tears over some truly wormy sins, but the ash crosses on their foreheads bade one and all to ponder the penances they might perform to grow in grace. Margaret considered washing more peasant's feet and giving alms to all who needed aid. She mostly hoped to face the devil as Jesus did in the desert and not succumb to his wiles.

As it turned out, Edward's caravan needn't have wasted time considering their Lenten wanderings, for the very real state of losing their way was provided for them only a few days later. And they nearly lost everything.

It was time to depart the hustle and bustle of Regensburg, but they were unsure which direction to take for next leg of the journey. Edward and his advisors were shown many maps, crude drawings really, of castles and abbeys and ancient roads, and the options Edward had to wade through were numerous and all seemed unnervingly vague.

He spent hours stroking his beard, trying to decide which option seemed viable. He knew that to continue traveling by barge on the Danube would leave them in the uncharted tangles of the Black Forest. So, after much discussion and not a little argument, he reluctantly agreed to portage the party northwest, picking up the Rhine River at Mainz, and hopefully arriving Cologne in time for Easter. If the weather held and they didn't get lost, the plan was feasible.

Three sets of guides offered to lead the party safely to the Rhine. Edward decided to trust some Benedictine monks because they spoke in specific, glowing terms about the beautiful cathedral in Mainz and St. Alban's, where they claimed they'd lived for a while. When he told Agatha of his choice, she looked away, uncertain.

"Don't do that to me, Agatha. You were in the room. You saw. You heard. Everyone had maps with pictures on them. Everyone talked about 'more dangerous' this and 'less treacherous' that. On what should I have based my decision? Tell me where I'm wrong and I'll change it."

"I don't know, Edward. I'm as confused and concerned as you are. I did think that perhaps the traders had made the passage before and remembered the way, but their maps were so tattered, I wasn't even sure which Duchy I was looking at. I think you made the right decision. We'll pick up local guides along the way."

But a few days later on the road, both Edward and Agatha were tamping down fears that they were hopelessly lost. The monks argued every night, pointing and drinking and arguing some more until ultimately, they simply drank the night away and were hungover the next morning, squinting painfully at the rising sun, poking their walking sticks aimlessly in the dirt for remnants of Roman cobblestones. Margaret didn't think anyone in the camp still believed they knew where they were going. By mid-morning, the men would simply shrug their shoulders, point randomly, and travel would commence in that general direction. Equally troubling, the caravan never crossed paths with anyone along the way. Edward's security detail was starting to look nervous. They closed ranks alongside him and rearranged the order of the riders to fortify their protection.

And now they were sleeping on the road, eating their own provisions. There hadn't been signs of a castle, abbey or village since they left Regensburg. Worse, their livestock seemed to be disappearing. Edward couldn't tell if he were simply imagining it, or if the animals were wandering off, or were being picked off by the wolves they heard howling nightly, or heaven forbid, being deftly stolen, one or two at a time ... by whom?

It was early one morning, right after Mass, as Margaret was riding with Cristina and Edgar within a cluster of soldiers, that Unwin silently pulled up beside her and took the reins from her hands. He'd been drinking. She could smell ale thick as old stew on his breath. It made her uncomfortable. He led her and her mount into the middle of a group of husky kitchen workers, where her tiny frame could scarcely be seen. He then got Edward's attention and pointed at her. Edward immediately had the other two children led away. Then he wheeled his horse around and rode off, Margaret assumed, to find her mother, whom she hadn't seen in two days.

Unwin abruptly left for the woods with a hunting party. She watched him take a big swig of ale, wiping his mouth with his sleeve, before going. The Unwin she'd come to trust had fallen back into his wicked ways, and it scared her. She prayed for his salvation, for hers and for her family's, for something was very wrong.

CHAPTER TWENTY-FOUR:

The Attack

---

*T*HE travelers stopped to eat. They were quite sure that it was about the sixth hour and that the sun was overhead, but it was hard to tell exactly where the sun was, given the gray clouds overhead and the thick brush that had closed in on them with increasing density. The horses were covered in insect bites and had bloody nicks crisscrossing their legs from brambles. They were dreadfully uncomfortable, in need of care and showing signs of balking. Whatever lay ahead, the horses were unsure whether or not they wanted to proceed.

For the first time on the journey, no one dismounted to eat, confusing Margaret, who desperately wanted out of the crush of kitchen workers surrounding her. One of the cooks offered her a bite of bread and meat. She refused, standing up in her saddle as tall as possible, but still couldn't see over their heads.

"Please, may I go eat with my siblings," she begged. "Why are you trapping me here? Am I in prison? Where's my mother?"

She was immediately hushed by several workers. She pursed her lips together to stay strong.

Distraught though she was, Margaret, so in tune with nature, was perhaps the first to notice the change: the world had gone unnaturally silent. The birds weren't chirping. Not a rodent stirred. Not a horse pawed the ground. The breeze that moments ago blew through the bushes, was still. For one long, terrifying moment, the world around them held its breath.

Then all hell broke loose. Blood-curdling war cries surrounded the caravan. Wild-eyed men in country clothing burst from behind bushes, wielding knives and clubs and running straight at the guards, while others fell like overripe fruit from tree branches carrying large sacks in their hands, running toward the most vulnerable wagons.

The English knights cursed and yelled, quickly dismounting to hold the robbers at bay with wide swings of their swords.

Someone pulled Margaret down from her horse. A massive pair of strong arms wrapped around her, carrying her to the innermost kitchen transport and shoving her inside a pitch-black wagon. A male voice boomed over the chaos, saying in Hungarian, "Hide in the cauldron."

She did as she was told, even as sounds of the struggle swirled closer to her hiding place. Horses' neighing told her that the Hungarian equestrians were setting formations to block the robbers' escape.

Margaret was in shock. She sat in the pot, shaking in the dark, trying to make sense of what was happening outside. How had these criminals found them? She'd heard of travelers being attacked on the road, but never a party this large, and with so many soldiers.

It dawned on her that her father's contingent had antici-pated this attack. She hadn't thought about it until now, but it did make sense: they were a rich group of travelers journeying slowly through the wilderness, wandering, with no idea where they were, or whether they were moving toward the Rhine River. They hadn't seen anyone else in weeks, but they lumbered along with wagons after chariots and chests, all holding enormous wealth. Truth be told, they were a soft and desirable target.

She could hear the royal contingent fighting back with increasing fury. Even the kitchen workers had entered into the fray. She heard them swinging iron hooks, throwing utensils at assailants and hacking at the air with kitchen knives. Crouched inside the cauldron, her pounding heart was making her chest bounce. She prayed to Saint Michael for protection for everyone.

Without warning, something sharp stuck her in the ribs. She cried out in pain and quickly yanked the weapon away from her unknown assailant. Who had found her?

But there was no one at the other end of the weapon, and she hadn't heard any footsteps. Puzzled, she gingerly examined the weapon with her fingers in the dark. It was oddly shaped. She banged it against the side of the pot. Its metal blade was strong and smooth, but not as flat as a blade should be. She placed it in her lap to feel the spot where the blade had poked her torso. She was unhurt. That was all that mattered for now.

She was becoming more confused than afraid. Furthermore, she realized the pot she sat in wasn't empty, but was lined with utensils at the bottom. She clutched the attack weapon, in case she needed it, while she tried to decide what to do. She wished she could look at it in the light.

Think, Margaret. You have choices. That's what Father says.

The wagon rocked back and forth. Now she was terrified, for someone evil had definitely jumped onto its side. The kitchen staff was screaming at the assailant, hurling iron utensils at him. A hail of large spoons must have forced him to let go because he screamed as he hit the ground, where the attack on him continued. He was trying to get away from the kitchen staff, and they began taunting him. They sounded as though they were enjoying playing with the miscreant.

"I'm eating you for dinner tonight, pagan."

"Don't! He must taste like the devil."

"Then I'll cut him into bite-sized pieces and feed him to the dogs."

"No, let's eat his flesh off the bone with lots of pagan sauce."

Margaret wondered if this triumph meant the robbers were retreating. There was a lull, and she heard cheers rising from parts of the camp. She peeked over the side of the pot, straining to hear her father's voice, but all she could hear were orders from the guards to remain vigilant.

She debated. Should she stick her head of the wagon and see the results of the attack for herself? What family treasures had been stolen? Had anyone been killed? Where was her family? She heard the whimpering of injured guard dogs and shouts for help to move a badly wounded man. Obviously, the bandits had had some success. Surely, they were gone now, she thought. But she'd wait just a bit longer.

A thought struck her. Those "guides" they'd picked up in Regensburg. They had to be the culprits. If they were responsible for leading them into this ambush, she wondered where they were. I hope the guards have killed them, she thought. Such evil couldn't be tolerated.

She listened intently but couldn't decide if the attack was over. She couldn't bear not knowing if her father was hurt. What about her mother and siblings? What would it mean to the throne of England if the worst had happened to her family?

She sat back down in her cauldron with the realization that even her survival meant something. Not as much as her father's or mother's, or even Edgar's, since he was heir to the throne, but she was a target, too. She'd never given it much thought before. Now she understood why the soldiers had separated the children when they realized there was danger. For now, she'd be quiet and stay put until someone came to get her.

She sat back down and felt around her for that weapon she'd been stabbed with. It was a mystery, but where was it? She groped in the dark until she found it and picked it up by its strange hilt. Odd. The blade was squared off and the tip was blunted. It made no sense.

Starting at the blade end of the "knife," she ran her fingertips lightly up part way, and stopped, trying to interpret the shape her fingertips were tracing. She moved her fingers slowly up and down until incredulously, she began to recognize a familiar figure in her mind's eye. The shape was Jesus on the cross.

She felt as silly as she did relieved, now that she understood what, rather than who, had stabbed her. This was a crucifix, and the more she thought about it, the more certain she was that it was one belonging to her father. It must have been in the pot, and she must have leaned against it in her panic. Jesus had been with her the whole time, saving her, when she'd thought someone was trying to kill her!

But what was a crucifix doing in a cauldron ... inside a kitchen wagon?

She'd assumed the bottom of the huge pot was filled with kitchen implements. Now, as she felt around for the objects under the blanket on which she'd been sitting, it took her breath away. Here were a number of tall and thin things. Candlesticks? They were beautifully shaped. Could they be altar candlesticks? Yes, they must be. In fact, she was sitting on all kinds of liturgical objects and vessels. She suspected there were even holy relics carefully buried in this holy trove. What were these folds of fabric? She gently ran her hand across the material. She'd rightfully guessed - these were embroidered priestly vestments.

Margaret took a deep breath. She'd been sitting on a fortune of holy items – crafted of gold and silver and precious stones – religious items that the bandits could have dismantled, melted down and sold for more money than they probably even knew. Her hiding pot was part of a brilliant plan to save her father's treasury, as well as to protect her.

She was too preoccupied in her astonishment to notice the sound of galloping horse hooves coming toward them again. When the guards sounded the alarm for everyone to prepare for another onslaught, she determined she'd protect her father's liturgical treasures with her life if she had to, and joyfully, because the sacrifice would be for her father.

"Lord Jesus, if I'm to be martyred, give me grace and please take me to heaven."

The intruders sounded close. Every soldier and nobleman in the caravan had his sword drawn. Just before the approaching party burst into the clearing, someone shouted, "Don't be alarmed. We're the returning hunting party. And we've captured the bandits!"

So they had, for all but Margaret to see. There were about thirty criminals, hands bound, many bleeding and all gasping for breath after being run back to the camp. Without their bravado, they all looked smaller and much less threatening to the travelers. At first, the Hungarians and Englishmen just stared at them. Then they broke into cheers, crying and hugging each other, for once, not caring who was from which country.

Riding in behind the camp's hunting party was a smartly uniformed military contingent.

"We're from Regensburg," their captain explained to the caravan. "We got word from some traders that a royal party had been fooled by men parading as monks. We'd never have found you if your hunting party hadn't been hunting for us. God was with you. We'll take these ugly faces back with us to Regensburg for justice."

Margaret now burst out her wagon, blinking in the light after being so long in the dark. She was disoriented at first by the sight of the mayhem left behind by the attack. Clothing, food, gold, broken chests, dying dogs, wounded horses and broken chariots littered the ground of what had been an ordered group of travelers. She stood, swaying, trying to make sense of what had happened around her, when Etel saw her.

"My good Lord, Margaret!"

Everyone turned to look at her. She was embarrassed by the attention, but even more concerned about her family.

"Where's Father? Mother? Cristina? Edgar?"

One of the hunters jumped from his horse and ran towards her, throwing off a broad-brimmed hat. It was her father.

"Darling Margaret, it's me. I'm right here."

He picked her up, tall as she was, and refused to set her down. Agatha, Cristina and Edgar came running in from the perimeter.

"We're here. We're all fine, Margaret," said her mother. "Etel and I stayed with the young ones. We knew you could handle being on your own. It was safer that we weren't all together."

"Father, where did you go?"

I went with the hunting party, partly to get help and partly to thwart the bandits' certain plan to kidnap me for ransom."

Edgar, who was unfazed by the event, announced, "And I had my sword, ready to defend everyone."

A ripple of laughter began, spreading person to person, releasing pent-up tension, until the entire camp roared with laughter. It confused Edgar, but he lapped up the attention.

In the midst of the ruckus, Unwin approached Margaret, hat in hand.

"I had to leave, under orders from your father. I didn't abandon you."

"I understand."

"I made sure you were safe. It was your father's idea."

"Thank you. It was a good idea."

"Were you frightened?"

"No. Yes. It was dark. I missed everything."

"You don't need to see evil's underbelly. Not yet, at least. Some day you won't be able to avoid it, but for you to see today's ugliness would have been like taking a rose and tearing the scent from it."

She looked at him, uncertain if he were serious. He looked at the ground and tried to explain.

"There aren't many good people in the world, Miss. Some are never good, some are born good, but life makes them bad, others are good only because they've never been tested, but some are born good and stay that way, no matter what happens. I guess it's the heart that the Lord gives them. Or their faith. I don't know, but you have goodness, Margaret."

She hardly knew what to make of him.

"Thank you, Unwin. I'll light a candle for you."

"I'd like that."

"Unwin?"

"Yes, Miss?"

"Your drinking ... you were drinking a bit ... no, you were drinking a lot ... when I saw you ride off with the hunting party. I was worried about you."

Hanging his head, as he did whenever his emotions got the better of him, Unwin said, "I had to be drunk enough, before I could bear to leave you behind. I was very worried about you."

CHAPTER TWENTY-FIVE:

Nyék's Redemption

---

*T*HE city of Regensburg rolled up its sleeves to patch together Edward's embassy. The wounded, some with cuts, bruises, broken bones and others with more serious injuries, were well-cared for. Over all, the losses had been remarkably minimal. Three dogs had been killed and one packhorse had to be put out of its misery. The injured horses were pampered, and they responded quickly. There were no human fatalities. The party was fortunate to have anticipated the attack in the nick of time.

Although people reported missing items, most of the bandits' haul had been found on them when captured and returned to the rightful owners.

A special Mass of thanksgiving in Regensburg gave Margaret the chance to rejoice that her family was safe. She was still praying after Mass when her father nudged her.

"Aren't you finished yet?"

He tried to look serious.

She blessed herself with the sign of the cross.

"Now I am."

They strolled into the sunshine.

"So, Margaret, did you feel close to the Lord during the ambush?"

She put her hands on her hips, feigning petulance.

Edward mirrored her stance and asked, "I don't even get a smile out of that?"

"I thought I'd been stabbed."

Edward was puzzled.

"What do you mean, stabbed?"

"I guess I leaned against your crucifix when I was in a panic."

He threw back his head and laughed, but when he saw the serious look on her face, he knelt down, cupping her face in his hands.

"My beautiful daughter. Before we even left Castle Réka, I gave much thought to my family's safety. There were plans made, and alternative plans and emergency plans beyond that. Every day of this trip is a risk because of who I am and the treasure we're transporting. We've tried to take every precaution we could think of."

"I understand, Father."

"You may understand many things beyond your years, Margaret, but no, you don't know what it feels like to have to protect your family. You were hidden today in the safest spot I could come up with, surrounded by a kitchen staff that would have died for you. If I sat you on top of holy treasures, well, I was asking the Lord to watch over you, even as you watched over what is His. You are pure of heart and I knew He'd hear your prayers."

"But I'm not pure of heart, Father."

"Next to the rest of us, you shine a little brighter, dear one."

"I'd give my life for you, Father."

He shook his head.

No, please don't. You mustn't think that way. It's my job to give my life for you. Give your life, if you must, for the Lord, or for those weaker than you, may you never have to, but don't ever give your life for me."

He stood, placing his hand on her head.

"You, my pious, maddening, lovely child, you did well during the raid."

"It was very dark in the wagon."

"Being left in the dark isn't always a bad thing." He paused for her reaction. "Aha! I made you smile."

She wiped the smile off with the back of her hand and marched toward her siblings.

"Too late," Edward called after her, a huge grin on his face. "I already saw it."

That day, the royal family made a point of visiting those who had been hurt in the attack. Agatha was shocked to find Nyék among the injured. His face was horribly swollen, and his arms were gashed, and blood seeped through his bandages.

"What happened, my friend?"

He tried to answer Agatha, but his lips were too swollen to move.

"Eh – en."

Agatha called over an attendant.

"Do you know the story behind his injuries?"

"I've no idea. He was attacked by one of the bandits, like everyone else here, Ma'am."

Nyék gestured painfully, moving his arms as though carrying something.

"Eh – en."

"Edward, please come here?"

Agatha motioned him over. Margaret trailed after him.

"Oh, no," said Edward.

"Nyék," cried Margaret. She knelt at his side and began praying.

"I can't understand what he's saying, but I thought you might," said Agatha.

"Eh – en," said the tutor.

A soldier further down the row scoffed.

"I heard the old man was running away when a bandit whacked him across the mouth."

Nyék shook his head 'no,' with a horrified look on his face.

Again, the tutor slowly lifted his arms. He looked down as though reading.

"You were reading, and they hit you?" Edward couldn't make any sense of it.

"G – eh," he painfully curled his tongue, "l – en."

"G – eh – en. G – eh – len."

Agatha looked quizzically at him.

"Gel – len?"

Edward felt silly asking.

"A bandit named Ghellen whacked you with a book?"

Agatha gave up.

"It hardly matters at this point, Edward. I'm so sorry you were hurt, my friend, but I think you'll be fine. Come, Margaret."

Edward lingered. This seemed important to the old man.

"Keen An – doo."

"Keen Andoo? Keen … King … Andrew? Yes, I'm right? King Andrew and Ghel - len? No, Kehlen? This will be a miracle if I can ever put it together, but since it concerns King Andrew, I'll try. I do hear he's recovering well. Your research was a help, Nyék, because I was able to converse fluently with his doctors. Ghelan. Kaylen. Gaylen. Galen? Are you talking about Galen's volume on apoplexy? Because we recovered it in the bandits' loot. I was thrilled to retrieve it from the robbers. You were running away with the book to save it, weren't you?"

Nyék's eyes filled with tears of relief. At least Edward understood his efforts.

"And that's when you were struck, and the volume stolen. My friend, you are a true scholar, a soldier for knowledge, and I salute you."

It was the proudest moment of Nyék's life.

The caravan had to move on, to reach Cologne by Easter. The wounded hoped to rejoin them during their stay with the Holy Roman Emperor.

But this time, Regensburg's finest guides would lead the Exile's party to the Rhine River.

Just arriving at the river was a milestone achieved. The Rhine was calm and lovely. Edward and Agatha watched the nobles and their finest horses being loaded onto the flat-bottomed boat. The children watched nearby.

"It's beautiful," said Margaret. "What a blessed day, after what we've been through."

"Do you think Pál can ride on our boat?"

Cristina was ready to marry him, even though Pál was far from a king. She no longer cared. He thought she was pretty, and that's what mattered to her.

"We'll ask Etel," said Margaret. "Let's not bother our parents. I've been praying that this part of our journey is peaceful and easy. Shall we all say the *Pater Noster?*"

As it turned out, as Margaret gratefully remembered in later years, her time on the Rhine was the most peaceful experience on the whole trip. The scenery was striking, which offset the grumpy Lenten fasting everyone was enduring, although they made up for the boring food by feasting heavily on Sundays.

It was, however, also an expensive leg of the journey, for there were many tolls to be paid along the Rhine. As a Lenten penance, Edward decreed that, for each toll the treasury paid, every adult, including the royal couple, would place alms into Margaret's kitchen pot, to be distributed to the poor when they reached Cologne. There were no complaints, since most hoped to bring good fortune to themselves by appearing generous. The pot grew so heavy, two mules were added to the equine team to help pull the wagon along the shoreline.

For all of Rhineland's beauty, the days were flying by. The end of March was approaching, meaning that Holy Week was not far off. The group pushed themselves to cover more distance each day.

CHAPTER TWENTY-SIX:

Easter Forgiveness

*T*HEY arrived Cologne on March 30th, a day before Palm Sunday. The parade through the city was more subdued, more Lenten-appropriate – no peasants went ahead of the nobles and royalty to sing their praises, the horses wore only half the amount of tassels they normally wore, and most importantly, the party stopped at the cathedral to offer their kitchen cauldron collection of alms for the poor. The priests took some confessions in return, with Margaret and her family having first access. She came out of the confessional wide-eyed.

"I feel so much better. I hope I remembered to tell him all of my sins," she said. "My penance is beautiful: I'm to recite the Three Fifties three times while standing and then celebrate the canonical hours with my arms reaching toward God and genuflecting twelve times for each hour, done with diligent concentration on heaven."

"The Three Fifties?" Little Edgar had never heard of them.

"Oh, that's just the one hundred and fifty Psalms divided into three sections. I pray fifty Psalms, then kneel twelve times. Then I pray the next fifty and kneel twelve times, and then the last fifty."

"You have to do one hundred and fifty Psalms three times all the way through?"

"Yes, and I want to do it three times, as penance for my dreadful sins."

"What dreadful sins? I'm glad I'm too little for confession," said Edgar emphatically.

It was late afternoon by the time they reached the court of Henry IV, Emperor of the Holy Roman Empire, where they were warmly welcomed by the castle staff, toasted with fine wine, fed and allowed to retire early to sleep on feather beds without having to endure a formal welcome with the emperor first.

Exhausted though they were the next day, Edward and his family attended Palm Sunday Mass, marking Christ's triumphant ride into Jerusalem on a donkey. Holy Week had begun.

Margaret fell in love with the cathedral's Baptismal fount.

"Eight sides. It's an octagon. Isn't it lovely? May I please be baptized again? Easter is glorious! Cristina, did you know that Charlemagne was the first emperor of the Holy Roman Empire? Just think of the men who have held that scepter."

Unlike Charlemagne, though, the current emperor, Henry IV, was a mere child of seven years. Edward was summoned for an audience with him early on the morning of Holy Thursday. He wondered how to develop a relationship with a boy about Edgar's age. I could, he thought wryly, help him with his studies, or gift him with a boy's wooden sword.

As he entered the room, Edward nearly didn't notice the boy sitting in his chair. He was swallowed up in its size. His adult teeth were just beginning to poke through his gums, and his legs only starting to lengthen; however, it was obvious that Henry knew he was King and Holy Roman Emperor. For now, his power lay with those around him, but it wouldn't be long before he asserted himself. Edward could sense it. The boy had soldiers standing at attention on either side of him and an overseer in the corner.

"I vaguely remember Bishop Ealdred's visit," said Henry, picking idly at a pile of grapes. "I was very young, but I remember he was an unpleasant man. I kept wishing he'd go home. My mother, the regent, tells me that Father knew all along that you were in Southern Hungary, but frankly, he didn't want you on the throne of England. He was very bitter about his military defeats in Hungary, and he had no intention of letting you be crowned. Me? I don't care much about that God forsaken country, so I promised mother I'd entertain you with kindness."

"Thank you, Sire. My condolences on losing your father."

"Don't be sorry. You wouldn't be sitting here with a beating heart in your chest, if he were still alive."

"Then shall we leave the past in the past and hope that the two of us can look to a future benefitting the Holy Roman Empire and England, as well as defending the pope and Rome?"

"Mother is working to get on the pope's good side. You can talk to her about things like that."

The doors were opened, and in walked Agatha with Agnes of Poitou, Henry IV's mother and regent. Edward noted how at ease the women were with one another. It was a good sign. Agatha was working her magic.

"Agatha, you're as pretty as Mother said, for an older woman," said Henry. "You can thank her for convincing me to welcome you. But you've come during Holy Week, when it seems we're always at the cathedral. I'll be too busy to see much of you, but you're here, so enjoy yourselves."

"You are most kind to us," said Edward, with a small bow.

"You must meet their children, Henry. Exemplary. They have two eligible daughters and a son about your age. I think you might want to consider their eldest daughter, my dear. She carries herself like an angel."

"Then I'll look for a girl carrying herself like an angel during the Washing of the Feet, which disgusts me anyway. I would never wash someone's dirty feet. You are all dismissed. We will see you at the Evening Mass of the Lord's Supper."

The ancient Great Three Days, the *Triduum*, were Margaret's favorite three days of the year. She immersed herself in them, literally feeling as though she sat alongside Jesus during the Last Supper, living through His scourging and enduring His death on the cross at Golgotha. She had to let her imagination run wild to imagine what opening the doors of hell was like, but she just knew the Resurrection had to be filled with more joy than she could imagine. She couldn't wait to feel it during Saturday night's Easter Vigil.

Getting dressed for these holy days took a long time for Margaret. She pulled out all her finery from the trunk, draping it across her bed in piles. She wouldn't wear her brand-new Easter outfit until Sunday morning, which left Thursday, Friday and Saturday to prepare for.

Etel left Margaret to her own devices. Over the last year, the girl had developed an uncanny sense of fashion, surpassing even her mother's. Etel watched Margaret harmonize colors first, boldly here, subtly there, and next playing with textures – silk with fine wool, a touch of fur for warmth and to frame the most important layer, and finally explosions of embroidery throughout, calculated to pull the eye carefully through the whole outfit.

The girl may be pious, thought Etel, but she also possessed a developed and very human streak of vanity. She wondered if Margaret was succumbing to the pleasures of the world.

When Margaret was finally ready, she couldn't have looked more perfect. Cristina stared at her with envy, but although Etel had tried her hardest to flatter the younger sister's brown hair and olive skin, it was impossible to make her as striking as Margaret, who attempted to make her sister feel beautiful.

"Cristina! Won't Pál have trouble concentrating during Mass! His eyes will be fixed on you. I can see my reflection in your shiny hair, and your eyes are the color of chestnuts. They'll glow in the Paschal candlelight, for sure."

"Thank you, Margaret. You look nice, too," said Cristina, who really wanted to believe her sister.

The family entered the cathedral formally, and in order of age, with Edward, Agatha, Margaret, Cristina and Edgar drawing much attention from the locals. Henry IV and Agnes of Poitou nodded to the *aetheling* when they entered the cathedral last, signaling the start of Mass. Henry noticed Margaret, but was more interested in Edgar, not as a playmate, but as a potential rival. He didn't want to have any more to do with the family. He'd leave that to his mother.

The next day was Good Friday. Margaret dressed herself in shades of brown and soft green, for the wood of the cross.

She cried during the reading of the Passion and sobbed as the cross processed to the altar. Those near her wept to see the child's devastation. She seemed too young to feel so deeply. By the time the priests shrouded the cross and the corporal, the consecrated wafer, and carried them out of the cathedral, she was too depleted to feel anything but the emptiness of the crucifixion and coldness of the sepulcher. She knelt quietly until her mother smoothed her hair.

"Let's go rest for the remainder of the day. Even Jesus rested, Margaret."

But by Saturday evening, Margaret had revived and was excited again.

"This is the night. Cristina! They bless the fire and the candle, the baptismal water is consecrated, the children are baptized, and the cantor sings the Gloria again!"

Poor Cristina was worn out.

"I don't know if I can stay awake."

"Don't worry, you'll wake up when the bells ring."

The cathedral shone with hundreds of candles. It was a night of joy, which Cristina enjoyed until sometime during the litany, which lulled her to sleep. Edgar didn't even make it that far. Margaret, on the other hand, couldn't get to sleep that night, because she'd been utterly entranced by the glowing, flickering wicks and smoky incense. She was thrilled to receive communion for the second time in one year; by the magnificence of the priests' robes as they processed into the church; and by a hymn she'd never heard, *Inventor rutili,* sung by two young boys. Their angelic voices echoed in her ears all night. She'd never heard anything so beautiful.

If by Easter Sunday most people had run out of energy, Margaret had hardly slowed down. She attended Easter Mass dressed as brightly as a bouquet of flowers, and she was a chatterbox afterwards.

"Mother, I've never seen so much gold on the altar! Nor have I seen a play performed at Easter service, have you? The deacons did such a good job playing the women at the sepulcher. It may be the most beautiful thing I've ever seen at Mass."

"I've never seen that before, either. It's a good idea. I liked it, too."

Agatha was as exhausted as the rest of the parishioners.

"I think I'm going to nap when we get back," she said.

"Is it alright if I take a walk? There a small forest at the edge of town."

"If that's restful to you, yes. But please tell Unwin where you're going. He'll stay a respectful distance away."

As it turned out, the two strolled among the trees together.

Unwin was curious.

"Why do you like praying by trees and streams so much?"

"Because everything outdoors quivers with life. It breathes. It's fresh. Indoors, the air is heavy and stale. What was once a tree is a dead wall. What was a happy rabbit has become trim on my shoes. But out here, everything is growing, whether fast or slow. I even think the rocks are growing, but too slowly for us to see. The water in a stream is always moving, changing, and changing everything it touches. The sun dances across the sky. The stars are a giant puzzle, moved by Mother Moon. I think everything has the Holy Ghost in it, don't you?"

"Yes. You say it prettier than I can, but that's why I like being a soldier. We're outside most of the time and I like watching the seasons and the sunrises."

"What about getting killed? Aren't you ever afraid?"

"I don't think about it. It's when you think about it that you die. I've seen it happen over and over. A man's eyes cloud over when he thinks about dying before a battle and it draws the arrow to him. So, I never let myself think about it."

"You know I want to forgive you, Unwin. I've thought it many times. I've never said it, but it's Easter and it's time. I forgive you for the way you acted. I'm sure the Lord does too."

"I've acted horribly so many times when I drink too much, Miss, that I'm not sure which time you're forgiving me for?"

"I'm talking about the first day we met."

"Oh."

He flushed with embarrassment. Margaret didn't notice.

"You scared me by saying horrid things. You were very drunk."

"With me, being drunk and horrible go together. I'm ashamed it happened. I was hoping you'd forgotten."

"I can forget about it, now that I've forgiven you. When you have enough love for someone, it's no longer difficult to forgive them."

"I would never hurt you on purpose. You're like my daughter."

"You have a daughter?"

"I don't think so. At least none that a woman can pin on me."

Margaret sighed.

"I suspect you've sinned, then. I hope you repent someday."

"I think it's just the life of a professional soldier. I promise you, I never thought I'd be friends with the likes of you." He realized he stepped over a line. "Forgive me, Margaret, I shouldn't have called you a friend. There I go being rude again, and I'm sober."

"Of course, we're friends. I don't have that many friends, you know, so I have to take care of the ones I have."

"I don't understand. Everyone says they adore you, and they talk about how beautiful they think you are. How can you say you don't have many friends?"

"Well, I'm neither amusing nor a sparkling conversationalist. Edgar says I'm boring, but he's barely six. Mother said once that I appear fragile and serious, and people aren't sure what to do with me. But I'm not fragile, although perhaps a little serious."

"You're going to be a strong queen."

"A strong nun, I hope. God willing."

"God willing."

They walked slowly, not talking much more, enjoying the sounds and scents of the forest as the sun set on Easter Sunday of a most eventful year.

CHAPTER TWENTY-SEVEN:

Soldier of Knowledge

*A*S the group readied for the final push to England, some of those less injured during the confrontation with the robbers arrived from Regensburg to rejoin the journey.

Margaret walked among them, welcoming them back and asking about Nyék. She questioned several Englishmen, but none of them knew who he was. She finally found a member of the Hungarian contingent.

"My tutor. You know. Is he here? Or is he still recovering?"

Another nobleman from Pécsvárad overheard her question.

"Are you talking about the old man with that story about the volume he was protecting?"

"Yes, the Galen volume. He was hit in the face."

"Milady, sweet girl, he was an old man. I regret to tell you, he got a gathering inside his mouth, a big pocket of pus that gave him great heat."

"What are you saying?"

"He didn't have the strength to fight off the fever. He shook and sweated for a day or so, and then he ..."

She blanched. The nobleman spoke more gently.

"I'm so sorry. The Lord called him home."

Margaret was speechless. It couldn't be true. But it was.

"Thank you for telling me."

"May God have mercy on his soul."

"Yes. May the angels lead him to heaven."

They held a special Requiem Mass for Nyék. Edward formally created the order of "Soldier of Knowledge," awarded it to Nyék and placed a special wreath on his coffin. Margaret plucked four flowers from the wreath, giving one to each of her siblings and tucking the third into her box with the feather and the white stone, so she would never forget him.

The fourth flower was for Ludmila, to enclose in the letter she'd write about Nyék's death. Ludmila's grief would be deep.

CHAPTER TWENTY-EIGHT:

An English Welcome

$\mathcal{T}$RAVELING from Cologne through Aachen and Ghent was a blur. People were weary of parading through towns, so Edward declared there would be no more parades until they reached London. The caravan was closing in on England and it was all anyone could think about, anyway. As tired as they were, excitement was mounting.

They stopped in Bruges for a brief rest and final preparations. Clothes were washed, people bathed and washed their hair and the horses were groomed to within an inch of their lives.

Etel interrupted Margaret's Anglo-Saxon lesson one morning.

"Margaret, your father wishes to see you shortly before lunch."

"Did he mention playing chess, I hope?"

"He did not."

Disappointed, Margaret nonetheless quickly changed into nicer clothes and braided her hair.

In her excitement, she arrived early, but when she knocked, a guard opened the door and Edward waved her in.

"Come sit. I'm having some food brought to us. Are you ready for London? I probably won't see much of you children for a while."

"I know. I've talked to Cristina and Edgar about it. We'll be fine, Father. We're proud of you."

"I have something important to share with you. I've been waiting for the right time, and I believe this is it."

Intrigued, Margaret sat up in her chair.

"I thought maybe we were going to play chess."

"No time for a good chess match today, but as soon as we're settled in London, I'll destroy you."

"Not if I destroy you first."

Their food was carried in on a silver platter. She ate only a few bites before Edward motioned her closer. She put down her food. The guard pulled her heavy chair next to her father.

"I've spoken to you many times about my hero, King Stephen of Hungary," began Edward. "He changed the course of history by converting the country to Christianity. I don't expect to exceed his accomplishment, but I hold it up as an example. Nor do I believe I can exceed his ability to capture wisdom in the written word, and so I hold up what he wrote to his son as a fine example of wisdom. Do you follow me?"

"Yes, Father."

"Before his beloved son Emeric was killed in a hunting accident, Stephen wrote letters of counsel for him. I can't present this advice any more eloquently than he did. What I'm reading to you today are the words he wrote, which I hope you'll imprint on your heart, because they come from mine. Let them guide you."

He pulled out a sheet of parchment. He had copied the words in his own hand for her to keep.

"This is what I wish for you to remember."

He read:

"My beloved son ..."

Edward paused.

"Or, 'my beloved daughter,'" he said, smiling. Then he began reading again.

"My beloved son, delight of my heart, hope of your posterity, I pray, I command, that at every time and in everything, strengthened by your devotion to me, you may show favor not only to relations and kin, or to the most eminent, be they leaders or rich men or neighbors or fellow-countrymen, but also to foreigners and to all who come to you. By fulfilling your duty in this way, you will reach the highest state of happiness. Be merciful to all who are suffering violence, keeping always in your heart the example of the Lord who said: 'I desire mercy and not sacrifice.' Be patient with everyone, not only with the powerful, but also with the weak.

Finally, be strong lest prosperity lift you up too much or adversity cast you down. Be humble in this life, that God may raise you up in the next. Be truly moderate and do not punish or condemn anyone immoderately. Be gentle so that you may never oppose justice. Be honorable so that you may never voluntarily bring disgrace upon anyone. Be chaste so that you may avoid all the foulness of lust like the pangs of death.

All these virtues I have noted above make up the royal crown and without them no one is fit to rule here on earth or attain the heavenly kingdom."

"That's it, Margaret. You will have fulfilled my every wish if you follow King Stephen's advice. When you're so scared, or confused, too confused to think or even to pray, take out this sheet of paper and read it and you'll know what to do. I was going to wait until your birthday to give this to you, but once Edward the Confessor formally proclaims me his successor to the throne, my time will not be my own."

"It's a good early birthday present. I'll do my best to make you proud."

"I know you will. Now, let's eat. Being wise makes me hungry."

Margaret laughed.

"Just thinking about being wise makes me hungry."

"Or, if you're Edgar, thinking makes you hungry."

"Breathing makes Edgar hungry, I think."

"Regarding Edgar … I will give him a copy of this when he's old enough … but remind him now and then, when he's grown, especially if he succeeds me, about the importance of these virtues."

"I promise."

The air was ripe with promise as the English and the Hungarians in the party, equally relieved to be this close to their destination, traveled south to the fishing village of Calais, their point of departure for England.

"I've a surprise for you: we're already in England," Agatha told the children. "Even though the people here speak Flemish, this land belongs to England."

"We did it," said Edgar, jumping up and down. "We're in England!"

"It won't feel like it to me until we're in London," said Cristina.

"We'll cross these waters to Dover Narrows, and then we'll truly be in England."

The sight of the steep, white cliffs of the Narrows drew gasps. They were stark, dramatic, and white as lamb's wool as they surged up from the blue waters, looking to the newcomers as though they'd been painted white.

The ships hugged the coastline, heading north to the mouth of the Thames. Margaret's heart soared. She wasn't certain if it was the intense beauty of the cliffs, or the reality that what she was finally seeing was their new home. Her father would be king of these cliffs, that hill, and all the cities and villages they were about to see, when the Confessor died. And she would become a princess. She now felt at least open to the possibility. She'd placed her faith in the Savior, whichever way His path led. She trusted Him to take her and her family to His goodness. The Lord is my shepherd, she thought. She let the sea breeze spray salt on her face.

Abbot Alwyn celebrated a special Mass at the bow of the family's vessel.

"Our intention in today's Mass is for our impending arrival at the end of a long journey. We offer it with our thanks to Him for the hospitality we've been shown along the way and for the strength He gave us to survive our difficulties. May the Lord bless Edward, lend him wisdom, give him peace, and protect him. Amen."

Margaret added her own prayer, in her head, one for Nyék's soul. She prayed that he wouldn't spend long in purgatory – that his soul would swiftly be taken up to heaven.

"He was prideful, Lord, but he worked hard to teach us what he'd been taught, even if it wasn't always accurate. And don't forget that he was willing to sacrifice his life to save my father's book, which was very brave. Please have mercy on him. Amen."

She leaped for joy when they found themselves on the Thames River.

"This is it, Cristina," said Margaret, wrapping an arm around her little sister. "Here we are, on the last leg of the trip. I've asked Mary to pray with us for a warm welcome from the English."

Edgar pointed.

"Look!"

He had spotted them first. People. They were running to the river, lining its banks, a few at first, waving and cheering. But as word of mouth spread faster than the boats, the crowds grew larger and more boisterous.

The children waved back to them. It was fun.

"Hello, England!"

"Hello, everyone, we're here!"

Cristina looked around.

"Where are Father and Mother? The people want to see them."

"I suspect," said Margaret, "they'll wait until we're closer to London."

But the people began chanting, "Edward! Edward!"

"Oh, my goodness," said Margaret, "look at the musicians on the banks – and the people are dancing. They're happy we're here. I can hardly believe it!"

Edgar danced to the music too, jumping and spinning, to the delight of the crowd.

The cheers grew louder, and a few minutes later, they became a joyful roar.

The children weren't sure why, at first, until they saw people pointing and waving at the bow. Agatha had appeared, looking stunningly like a queen. There was no mistaking who she was, and it was clear that England was already in love with her. She waved gently, but warmly, turning to both sides of the boat to embrace everyone with her smile.

Margaret was entranced by her mother's expansive presence at this moment. The image of Agatha embracing her new countrymen with fullness of grace and womanly dignity made an impression on Margaret. She thought about the admonitions King Stephen had written to his son Emeric and realized that this woman, her own mother, embodied those qualities in a way that only a whole-souled woman could. She wanted to be that as a woman, too.

Agatha turned. Edward was joining her. She bowed ever so slightly to him and held out her hand. He kissed it, put his arm around her waist and together they stood as one. It was a magnificent show of solidarity.

The people along the river went wild, singing songs and waving banners. Young men drinking ale from buckets raised toasts to the couple as they floated by. Old men who'd fought for England and remembered his father, Edmund Ironside, stood at attention before their future king, causing Edward to wipe away a tear on his sleeve. He was deeply touched by the outpouring of affection. He hadn't known what to expect, but he certainly hadn't expected this jubilation. It was profound encouragement for his future reign, and he swore to the heavens that he would do everything in his power to be worthy of it.

As they approached the center of London, the wooden houses that had sparsely dotted the banks were now built closely pressed together, so tightly that Margaret wondered how people breathed in them. Still, it was exciting to be in the city. People were standing shoulder to shoulder, in rows too deep for her to count. It seemed the whole city had turned out, craning their necks to catch a glimpse of Edward and Agatha.

Margaret saw much finger-pointing and head-nodding. She decided it was a very favorable reception. She was eager to meet her great-uncle, the Confessor and to witness his piety. She hoped he'd approve of her. She imagined that his court was pious as well. How could they not be? She definitely wouldn't expect to see girls like the Faded Nosegays at King Andrew's court. She doubted the Confessor's wife, Edyth of Wessex, would allow that, especially since she'd heard that the Confessor and Edyth had never consummated their marriage. If that were true, Margaret admired their chastity. She knew that too often, women lusted for sex more than men, in marriage and even more in widowhood. It was something she intended to guard against. If she had to marry, she hoped her husband would be as chaste as her great-uncle.

The boats docked quayside. Nearly three months of traveling were finally at an end. The English contingent surged onto the banks of the river, greeting friends and family who were happy to welcome them home. The Hungarians hung back, following the lead of the *aetheling* and enjoying the boisterous reception.

The king's troubadours stepped forward to sing songs about the Confessor and his worldwide search for his nephew. Then, for the benefit of the Londoners who might not know, they recounted the major events of Edward's exile.

"Did you know," said Margaret to her siblings, "that the Confessor spent years in exile, too?"

Etel, standing next to Edgar to ensure he behaved properly in front of the crowd, answered for them. "Yes, those twenty-five years in Normandy. Margaret, do you remember what I told you? The Confessor leans towards the French. He gives them too much power in his court and in the Church, and they're pleased to take it."

"I'm sure it'll be fine, Etel," said Margaret. "According to what King Stephen wrote, a good king is kind to people from other countries, not just his own."

"And a smart king," said Etel flatly, "doesn't allow foreign countries to whittle away at his power."

Edgar was fidgety.

"When will we meet King Edward?"

"Well," said Etel, "I'm sure he knows we've arrived. He may be in Winchester. I think it'll be another day or two. That's when we'll parade into London."

The Bishop of London, Robert of Jumièges, stepped forward wearing majestic vestments of gold thread and pearls, flanked by a dozen lesser bishops. Etel practically snorted.

"Do you hear that nasty French accent? There he is."

Edward, Agatha and the children stared at the English, even as the clergy and representatives of the English court stared back at them.

What the English saw was a family of foreigners wearing odd clothing, and their impression of Edward was of a middle-aged man who had gone into exile from Wessex shortly after his birth, and who was unable to speak English well enough to respond to their welcome. But because he was a rightful heir to the throne, with genuine Anglo-Saxon blood running in the veins, they also considered him the perfect candidate to be the next king of their country.

The family was escorted to beautiful country accommodations and presented with a feast of the finest English cuisine, most of which the children found rather unpleasant.

"The chicken tastes funny," Cristina whispered to Margaret.

"Please don't make faces, Cristina. It's rude," Margaret whispered back, poking her arm to make her stop wrinkling her nose. "We'll get used to it."

"I don't think so. It's a good thing I'm starving, or I couldn't eat."

"I fear there will be a lot of strange things to get used here. We may have to pretend to like things, when we don't. If you wish, I can teach you how to smile, even when you're not happy. I know how to do it, and it works, although I still don't understand why."

CHAPTER TWENTY-NINE:

A Pawn

JFOR the next four days, Edward and Agatha stayed close to the estate where the family was living. Edward wanted to be available to meet with the Confessor, and he expected to be summoned at any moment. After family Mass each morning, he spent his days walking the grounds with Agatha and receiving various local noblemen, some of whom he could converse with in Danish, and others with whom he utilized a translator, although Edward had the feeling that the translator's English to Hungarian was only roughly accurate. But any kind of translator was better than pointing, nodding, smiling and pretending to understand while in a state of bewilderment.

"Why don't you go riding, Father?"

Margaret knew he was restless.

"Well, the king is surely going to meet with me very soon to formally declare me his successor. I'm content to wait. He's probably counseling with the *Witangemot*."

"Counseling? About what? You're the blood heir. Is there anything else I should know about? What is there to discuss?"

Edward laughed.

"Precisely. I'm the only logical choice to succeed Edward, and the Confessor personally sent Bishop Ealdred to fetch me. Even our unpleasant bishop, assured me while we were in Hungary, that the king had named me his heir. I'm told the Confessor actually shed tears when he learned I was alive and well. But legally, the *Witan* get to have their say."

Five days went by without any word from Edward's court. Six days. Then a week. The unexpected wait was becoming maddeningly tedious.

On day eight, a neighboring lord pantomimed a bird in flight, swooping down to grab prey, a clear suggestion that they go hawking on his land, just down the road. Agatha thought it was a wonderful idea.

"I'll stay right here, Edward, and get word to you if you're summoned. You'll feel better after doing some hunting."

"You're right. And I'll stay close enough to respond quickly."

Edward's groom had his horse ready to ride. He settled himself contentedly into the saddle, allowing the week's idleness to slip from his shoulders.

He was joining a group of five local noblemen, each with his falcon perched on his wrist and his falconer riding alongside him. Edward's falconer brought his favorite Gyrfalcon from the mews and let her step onto Edward's arm. She chirped in happy recognition.

"Did you miss me, girl? Let's get your talons into some prey as soon as possible."

Inhaling the fresh air, the Exile looked around. The sun was gently excusing the morning fog's grayness, letting light shine through the mist onto the rolling terrain. He was already feeling better.

He slipped the hood from the falcon and sent her toward the sky. The hunting party took off at a gallop.

Edward realized how desperately he'd missed the pounding of his stallion's hooves into the ground beneath him, and the excitement of the animal's muscles flexing beneath him. Freedom. Life felt good again.

The peregrines were soon bringing down ducks from a flock that had picked the wrong place to fly.

Although the morning was still cool, Edward began wiping sweat from his forehead.

"I think I'm getting a fever," he said in Hungarian.

His fellow hunters stared quizzically at him.

He wiped his forehead again and slouched over to show he wasn't feeling well. Then he pointed in the direction of the house.

"I'm going back."

They nodded, making sympathetic gestures.

While his falconer tracked his bird, Edward headed back to the estate.

The groom was surprised to see Edward riding toward him. He was returning much too early. He also wondered why Edward's horse seemed to be meandering. He headed out to meet Edward, but as he got closer, he could see that Edward was listing to one side. The groom started running, but before he could reach him, Edward slid off his mount, hitting the ground on his stomach. The young groom hurried to aid Edward, whom he assumed was injured.

"Sire. Where do you hurt? Shall I stay with you or get help?"

Edward raised a hand to stop him from leaving. He gestured for the groom to roll him over on his back. He was drooling but tried to speak. As the groom turned him over, he saw that Edward was frothing at the mouth.

"Don't waste your energy on talking, Sire. Let me get help."

"No," mouthed Edward. He spit and cleared his throat. Then he whispered something. The groom leaned in closer.

"I'm sorry, I couldn't hear you. Please say it again, Sire."

"The saddle," Edward whispered. He held up his ungloved hand. It looked ugly – there were large blisters on his palm, and it was a fiery red. The white foam collecting at the corners of Edward's mouth was trailing into his ears. He whispered again.

"The saddle. Poison. Careful, you and the horse."

He coughed, spewing blood.

The groom was frantic.

"I'll get Agatha."

"No. Stay. Tell my family I love them."

"Who did this to you?"

Edward was weakening too quickly to talk anymore, and blood trickled from his nose. He shook his head. He didn't know who was to blame.

The groom was frantic to get him help.

"Stay with us, Sire. Please!"

He ran toward the house, screaming.

Left all alone, Edward gazed up at a beautiful blue sky. England. He'd waited forty years for his chance to rule. He'd come so very close. He wished for a priest to give him last rites, but long ago, he'd accepted that life didn't always work out the way you wanted. Of all people, he understood the difference between desire and destiny. Now his time was running out and he had to make a deathbed confession while his mind was still functioning. His last confession would be directly between him and his Maker. He mouthed the words as his strength failed.

"Lord, have mercy on me, for I am a sinner. Mary, pray for me. Christ have mercy. Forgive me my sins and receive me into your kingdom. I confess that I have sinned through my most grievous fault ..."

To his dismay, he started convulsing. No, he couldn't die yet, he had to confess his misdeeds. Would the devil steal his soul before he could offer it cleansed for the Lord? His mind was fading to gray, and Edward realized all he had left to offer was his faith. He let go of desiring mortal life, giving everything he was, the good and the bad, his strengths and his weaknesses, his love and his fear to his Lord. He must have been granted mercy, for his last breath fell softly from his lips.

By the time Agatha reached him, he was staring at the blue sky. She collapsed on the ground next to him, hysterical.

"Be careful, Milady. The poison may have spread from his hand. We don't know if he ingested some by accident, or if just touching it is lethal."

Servants and ladies-in-waiting were pouring out the front door.

"Keep my children in the house," Agatha called out. "They mustn't see him like this." She looked at the groom, disbelief in her eyes. "Who? Why? Who had access to the stables?"

The groom shook his head.

"People come and go all the time here. The owners of this estate have their own people taking care of the grounds. I see them daily, but I don't know who they are. I suppose someone could have pretended to be a worker and wiped poison on Edward's saddle as they walked by. It only takes a few drops to kill if the poison is strong enough."

Agatha gently closed her husband's eyelids and prayed the *Pater Noster.* Anger welled up inside of her.

"Someone didn't want him to sit on the throne. Curse the devil who did this. Go find the hawking party and tell them what's happened. If one of them doesn't seem to be surprised, I want to know which one it is. But regardless, ask them what we do next."

The hunting party returned in a gallop, looks of genuine horror on every face. The nearest neighbor peeled off to inform someone attached to the crown of the catastrophic event.

Agatha refused to leave Edward's side until representatives of the Confessor's court arrived a few hours later. They wore thick gloves to clean up the body, until it was presentable enough for the children to say goodbye. Etel had given them the news earlier, and their faces were already swollen and red from hours of crying. Etel held the two younger children's hands and led them to kneel beside their father, careful to shield them from touching him. Edgar snuffled. Cristina wailed.

Margaret held back, hesitating, until Agatha nodded to her, encouraging her.

"This is your last chance to tell him you love him."

Margaret set her jaw and approached her father, the hardest thing she would ever do in her life. But her eyes were dry. She sat on the grass and studied her father's face for a long time.

"It's such a sweet face, Mother."

"You're right, Margaret, it is."

Margaret cocked her head, thinking. Then she leaned over and whispered something in her father's ear, sitting back up with a smile on her face. Opening her hand, she placed the king piece from her favorite chess set on her father's chest.

"Mother, may this please be buried with him?"

"Of course, Margaret. I'll see to it."

Taking one final look at her father, she finally broke down. Tears streamed silently, unchecked, down her face. When she was ready, she walked over to Agatha, and wrapping her arms around her mother, let the would-be queen sob on her shoulder.

It was time for the men take Edward's body. Agatha knelt one final time and leaned over to kiss him on the lips.

"No, no, please don't, Ma'am."

"If you touch the poison, you could die as well."

"Don't you understand? I don't care if I die beside him here and now," Agatha said, kissing him again and again. "Goodbye, my darling Edward."

Agatha and Margaret remained behind even after the body was gone. They stood quietly together, just the two of them.

When the sun began to set on their most horrible day, they walked back to the house, arm in arm. The torches in the family chapel burned all night as the two women prayed for the man they loved most in the world.

The court of Edward the Confessor didn't sleep that night, either. The future of the English monarchy now lay vulnerable and subject to unexpected pressures and treachery. Certainly, someone knew how Edward the Aetheling died, but for now, their secret was secure.

Nothing else was certain – nothing, except that more violence was inevitable.

The news of Edward's death would travel quickly across the continent. The drums of war would soon begin to beat.

CHAPTER THIRTY:

Edward the Confessor

*T*HE morning of her father's funeral was cold and foggy, appropriate, Margaret thought, for this sad occasion. A week ago, England had represented a joyful new beginning. Today, it felt sinister, with evil hiding inside the city's gray mist.

Someone, or a group of people, had kept her father away from the Confessor until they could kill him; however, no one in all of London would publicly speculate who the murderer might be. Clearly, whoever the instigator was, he was immensely powerful because people were afraid to name him. The family couldn't know that behind closed doors, though, the two names being whispered the most were Harold Godwinson, a highly influential voice in the Confessor's court, and Duke William of Normandy, the bastard, and Edward's relative, living across the water, in France. He was a man convinced he held a claim to the throne.

The family arrived at St. Paul's Cathedral shortly before the Requiem Mass began. They were shocked to see the size of the crowd: London was in deep mourning for Edward. Apparently, their affection for the Anglo-Saxon heir had been genuine, as were their tears at losing him. It gave Agatha a bit of solace.

"Do you see their grief? They loved him. They know what a worthy king he would have been. May his murderers burn in hell."

Etel patted her hand. The children sat quietly.

Margaret forced herself to keep her mind filled with happy memories of her father during the Mass. Anything else was too painful. At one point, she let herself stare at his coffin that rested on the altar, but she didn't want to look at his body. She didn't think she'd recognize him. Even on the day he died, as she'd whispered in his ear, he hadn't looked like himself. She supposed it was because his spirit had already left its habitation, a dove flown home to heaven. That helped her, knowing that what they were burying in the cathedral were only remnants of his body, dust to dust ... still, she couldn't imagine never seeing him again for the rest of her life. It was a raw pain that would never leave.

Cristina leaned over to her.

"Tell me what you whispered in his ear that day?"

"It was only meant for Father. He heard me say it, too. I could tell."

"I couldn't think of anything to say."

"He knew you loved him. That's all he needed to know."

"Someday you'll tell me what you said."

"Maybe."

Margaret stayed deep in her own thoughts during the funeral. It was easier than becoming part of the weeping around her. The only time she faltered was when the choir intoned the *Dies Irae*, written by Pope Gregory the Great.

Dies irae, dies illa,

Solvet saeclum in favilla,

Teste David cum Sibylla.

Quantus tremor est futurus,

Quando Judex est venturus,

Cuncta stricte discussurus!

She translated the words as best she could in her mind, and they frightened her.

"Day of wrath and doom impending,

David's word with Sibyl's blending,

Heaven and earth in ashes ending.

Oh, what fear man's bosom rendeth,

When from heaven the Judge descendeth,

On whose sentence all dependeth."

She'd pray every single day for her father's salvation. But she pushed the fear of his judgment from her mind. Her father had been a good man.

She was relieved when the Mass was finally over, and they removed the coffin. She started to kneel again, to pray a little on her own, as she always did, when Agatha pulled her back up by her clothing, for standing before them was King Edward the Confessor himself and his entourage. The women curtsied and Edgar bowed.

It was the first time they'd seen him in person. Margaret was dumbstruck by his appearance. He was a very pale man, as though most of his blood had been drained, and his hair was very white. When he lifted his hand, she was surprised by their long, thin fingers and translucent quality. It was as though she could see his veins and bones right through the skin. He reminded her of the *albus* hart in the forest, with that same otherworldly look.

When he spoke to them, his regret seemed to be from his heart. His voice shook.

"I'm so sorry," said the Confessor. "This is a dreadful turn of events. Was Edward ill?"

He looked hopeful, for an illness would remove the stigma of an assassination.

"No," answered Agatha, looking him in the eye.

The Confessor shook his head.

"I should have seen it coming."

But he said no more. Apparently, even he didn't dare speculate about the culprits. But he had to have his suspicions or even know exactly who'd done it, thought Agatha. She wondered if he hadn't played a political game with her husband's life. She was beginning to wonder if the king had promised the throne to more than one man. But the Confessor was her only protector now and she needed his friendship.

Agatha pointed to her children.

"What do I do now?"

"I've given that much thought," said the Confessor, "and I give you my solemn pledge in this house of God that I will take care of you and raise the children as my own. I never had children, so it will be my pleasure to make them my responsibility; to see that they are educated and protected."

"Thank you, Your Majesty."

"As soon as you are ready, you will move into my court. Would you like to keep your Hungarian servants?"

"Yes. May God bless you, Your Majesty."

"I take your sadness personally. May the peace of God be with you."

Margaret's head was spinning. She'd assumed they'd be going back to Hungary, but apparently, this was to be their new life, here, in this strange country. At least, she reasoned, she could come visit her father's tomb whenever she wanted to talk to him.

The fog still lay thickly across London as they left St. Paul's, veiling their future from them. They had no clue what lay ahead.

"You always have choices, in chess and in life."

Her father's words rang in Margaret's head. He was right. She wasn't helpless, even though it would be easy for her to feel that way. But she had choices. She could choose how she lived the rest of her life. She vowed then and there to live a life of kindness, as King Stephen had urged his son to do; one that would make her own father proud of her. And she resolved that this adversity would not crush her, at least not for long.

Would she forgive her father's killers? Not now. She couldn't imagine she ever would, so maybe she wouldn't. She couldn't foretell if that day would ever come. Her dearest father been stolen from her and virtually expunged from history, as though he'd never existed. The thought left her weak with anger.

Yet somehow, a few days after turning twelve years old, Margaret of Wessex chose to turn her back on a devastating past. With all the courage she could muster, she chose to walk through life with her heart open to life's goodness.

All right, my dearest father, she thought. For now, I'll choose to be patient and strong. I'll never forget that I have choices.

CHAPTER THIRTY-ONE:

A poem from 1057

"Here comes Edward Aetheling

To Engla-land;

He was King Edward's

Brother's son,

Edmund king

Who Ironside was called

For his valour …

Nor wist we

For which cause

That was done,

That he could not

His kinsman Edward

King behold."

A translation from The Worcester Manuscript

Anglo-Saxon Chronicle, 1057

Translation taken from "The Lost King of England,"

BY GABRIEL RONAY

CHAPTER THIRTY-TWO:

The Beginning

WHETHER it was from remorse or true affection, King Edward kept his word. He brought Agatha and the children into his court, treating them as family. Agatha kept separate quarters, living among the Hungarians that had come with them from Castle Réka. She avoided the English court, for she couldn't bear to see its members, wondering each time she did, if she were looking at her husband's killer. His murder had broken her. All those years in exile, hoping and waiting for the call to the throne, had been for naught, vanishing the moment Edward touched the poisoned saddle. Agatha was too depressed some days to get out of bed. This was one of those days. Margaret sat next to her.

"Mother, you must eat, and here, let me open the curtains to let in some light. It's a lovely and sunny day."

"There are no more lovely days, Margaret. All those years, I prayed that your father would one day wear the crown. I prayed every single day. Why didn't the Lord answer my prayers?"

"I don't know, Mother. We're not allowed to know some things, at least not on earth."

Margaret's heart sank. The strong woman she'd always known could hardly be the same woman whose hand she now held. This woman had dark circles sagging beneath sunken eyes and had given up on life. Margaret stroked her arm. Her skin felt loose. She'd lost a lot of weight. Nothing brought Agatha joy these days. She moaned.

"It's over, our lives snatched away from us, and we're stuck in exile again, only this time, without any hope that our prayers will be answered."

"Our lives are not over, Mother. Edgar is still in line for the throne, and he's maturing every day. By the time the Confessor dies, Edgar could be old enough to rule, but if he's not, you could be his regent. You'd be the mother of the king, if not the wife of one, and you'd offer wisdom, which Edgar needs, because he is not the least bit wise yet."

Agatha almost brightened, then sighed and pulled the blanket over her head.

"This is not the way it was supposed to be," she snapped.

"That's it, Mother, get angry. Angry is better than sad. Anything is better than sad. Cristina, Edgar and I need you to get well."

"You children don't need me at all. I'm finished being a wife, mother and queen, but you have a life ahead of you. Leave me be, Margaret, and go live your life. Let me sleep, now."

Queen Edyth was waiting for Margaret outside the door. Eighteen years younger than her husband, the Confessor, her thirty-five-year-old eyes sparkled with intelligence. She appeared to Margaret to be everything a queen should be: cultured and polite, excellent at embroidery and weaving, but also conversant in Latin, French, Danish and Irish, as well as being learned in rhetoric, arithmetic and astronomy. Margaret was in awe of her.

Edyth, in return, saw herself in Margaret and had decided to mentor her shortly after meeting her. Margaret was easy to love.

"You're the daughter I'll never have," she'd told Margaret, only a week after Edward the Aetheling was buried. "I'll see to your education and your refinement. I only hope you'll love me like a mother."

That wasn't difficult for Margaret, except her affection for Edyth made her feel guilty, as though she had abandoned her real mother. Margaret was also curious as to why the king and queen didn't have children of their own. She'd heard that the king hadn't fathered any bastard children, nor had anyone ever mentioned Edyth suffering miscarriages. So then, why no children within the marriage?

Edyth must have sensed her curiosity, for one day she patted Margaret on the hand, saying, "The court buzzes with questions. Have you heard them whispering? Such gossip about children! 'Why doesn't he …' 'Why don't they …' 'Can he …' 'Can't she …?'"

"It's none of my business, Your Highness."

"It is your business if you're my 'daughter,' so I'm going to tell you. I respect our good and holy king as the father of England – and since I'm his subject as well as his queen, he's my father, too. We spoke about living chastely before marriage. We don't need to produce a personal heir. The *Witan* in their wisdom is charged with collaborating in choosing his successor."

Margaret furrowed her brow.

"But my father was the king's nephew and a direct heir …"

Edyth regretted her quick tongue, which sometimes blathered before she'd considered the ramifications of her words. Margaret didn't need to know that her father had been a compromise choice: too unknown for anyone to dislike him, yet a full-blooded Englishman and not a Norman, and also a relative with a claim to the throne. Nor did she need to know that Edyth's father, the powerful Earl Godwin, had demanded that Edward marry his daughter as a debt of gratitude for his support. Politics were complicated and Margaret wasn't yet old enough to understand the extensive influence the Godwin family had on the king's court, an influence that included input on choosing the next king.

"Exactly my point," she quickly replied, "Edward convened the *Witan* as soon as your father was discovered in Hungary, to tell them that the successor he'd been searching for had been found at last. I personally wiped tears from his eyes."

"That comforts me," said Margaret. "My father waited for so long to be worthy of the crown."

Edyth looked into Margaret's blue eyes. There was no guile in her, and Edyth loved her for it. Still, she changed the subject. The child would eventually learn the ways of the world.

"Come. I want to share with you the plans for rebuilding Wilton Abbey. This time, we're using stone. I'm tired of so many wooden abbeys burning to the ground. I won't let it happen to Wilton, our beloved school. I'll be forever grateful to the abbey for my education, and I'm going to ensure it stands forever."

"Your Highness, your generosity must please the Lord." She hesitated. "May I ask you a question? Do you find it wrong that most of us at Wilton don't have to wear habits? I fear we wear our vanity within the layers of our lovely clothes. And the lay sisters do everything for us."

"You mustn't feel guilty about who you are. The one Lord has one will, but it's performed by many hands, doing various tasks made obvious by our stations in life. Your tender hands were not made for tilling soil, Margaret. You're an aristocrat."

"Well, I'll change into the habit when it's time for me to follow the Rule of Benedict."

"Let's wait and see, my dear. We're not rushing you into anything and your talents are many. There's no need to think about it right now."

They entered the queen's chambers to see the plans for Wilton Abbey's rebuilding, which were beautiful, but what astounded Margaret more were the many relics the queen had in her private chapel. There seemed to be piles of them: small caskets, ornate boxes; miniature silver and gold cathedrals or even molded body parts, such as arms and heads. Edyth opened several of the reliquaries to let Margaret hold the sacred objects. Margaret was stunned to have St. Catherine of Alexandria's hair laid in her hands.

"I bought this in Venice. Someone must have cut this lock of her hair after they tortured her on the wheel that broke and Emperor Maxentius had to behead her to kill her."

"Didn't they bury her in Egypt?"

"Yes, but her relics have found their way around the world. Can't you feel the powerful grace in her hair? Think of what she went through, and she was only about seventeen."

"How long ago?"

"About seven hundred years. Margaret, it's vital that women like you and I collect these saintly objects. One can never have too many sacred relics. And it's important to share them, to inspire others to live and die for their faith. Most of these are for Wilton Abbey. Here is a nail from the true cross, brought all the way from Jerusalem. Go ahead, pray over it. Inside here is St. Augustine's finger. And here is the original Donation of Constantine. It's about seven hundred years old, too. See? He designates power to Rome right here."

"This must be your greatest treasure."

"No, there's one that we've buried under our altar and covered with the heaviest of stones."

"What's inside?"

"I'll tell you, but you must promise to protect the answer with your life."

Margaret swallowed hard.

"I promise."

"We have one of the infant Jesus' baby teeth."

"No. That's astonishing. How do you find such treasures?"

"Oh, every convent, monastery, or cathedral I walk into now, trembles when they see me coming, for they know they're about to lose one of their favorite relics. I have the money; I'm the queen and they know most of their relics will wind up at the most prestigious school for girls in the country. How can they say no? They may get upset, but that's not my fault. Oh, part of Mary Magdalene's cloak is right over there," she said, gesturing to a gold reliquary studded with stones. "I'd put that as our second-greatest treasure."

Margaret could barely breathe among the spiritual riches. They were overwhelming.

"My dear queen. I think I need some fresh air after seeing these holiest of holies."

"I know exactly what you need - a ride on one of your Hungarian horses. Am I right?"

"Oh, that sounds perfect."

"I've had one saddled up for you all day. I know you too well, Margaret. Like a mother."

Margaret couldn't help but think of her father as she hurried to the stables. She still missed him every single day, but nothing brought her closer to him than the freedom she felt galloping a horse across an open meadow. She leaped on her mount.

"Ut, Ut!" She shouted the war cry she'd uttered the day she and her father had eluded his guards. Once again, she wondered what her life would have been like had he become king of England. When Edward the Confessor died, who would take his place now? Would Edgar be prepared to wear his crown, or would there be a struggle for power? Would it be a smooth transfer, or would there be bloodshed?

"Ut, Ut!" She shouted again. She wouldn't think about it now. For now, she'd pretend her father was riding alongside her, the wind blowing in their hair, thinking only about each other, not caring about the world around them, only enjoying their freedom. She rode on, toward a rolling hill. She wondered if there mightn't be a small stream on the other side, where she could pray as she did when her life was simpler. She urged her mount up the incline, stopping to take in the view. It was a sweeping vista and her heart opened up, taking it all in.

She felt eyes burning holes in her back. She whipped her head around. Sitting astride his horse one rise away was Malcolm III. This time she was struck by his kingly manner. He no longer appeared shy and tongue-tied, but fiercely independent.

She smiled tentatively.

Placing a fist over his heart, he bowed his head. It was a noble gesture, but it caused him to miss the rabbit that hopped between his horse's legs. The steed spooked and reared.

Margaret held her breath. She did not want to see the king thrown from his horse. It would be too embarrassing to witness.

Luckily, Malcolm was a master horseman and he averted disaster, but his moment of chivalry had been ruined and it angered him. The King of Scots turned his horse and galloped away without a word. She'd see, he thought, in good time. He was off to Scotland in the morning, but the day would come when she'd get to know him … and then she'd see.

Well, thought Margaret. Queen Edyth was right. Despite the fact that she seemed to unnerve him, his gallantry and rugged masculinity were appealing. In that way, he reminded her of her father. She might come to admire this man, a man who likely would find a way to leave his fingerprints on the parchment of history. She wondered how she'd feel about him if he ever spoke to her. That day would come. And then she'd see.

4
2

SELECTED BIBLIOGRAPHY:

Abernathy, Susan. *Edith of Wessex, Queen of England.* June 5, 2012. thefreelancehistorywriter.com

Aelfric, Abbot of Eynsham. *The Homilies of the Anglo-Saxon Church.* "Project Gutenberg's The Homilies of the Anglo-Saxon Church by Aelfric." Translator: Benjamin Thorpe. Release date: December 18, 2011, (EBook #38334). http://www.gutenberg.org/files/38334/38334-h/38334-h.htm#page181

Barlow, Frank, Editor and translator. *The Life of King Edward the Confessor who rests at Westminster (Vita Aedwardi Regis).* Oxford: Clarendon Press, 1992. Print.

Barnett, T. Radcliffe, Ph.D. *Margaret of Scotland: Queen and Saint, Her Influence on the early church in Scotland.* Edinburgh: Oliver and Boyd, 1926. Print.

Brooke, Iris. *English Costume from the Early Middle Ages Through the Sixteenth Century.* Mineloa, New York: Dover Publications, Inc., 2000. Print.

Chibnall, Marjorie. *Anglo-Norman England: 1066-1166.* Oxford: Basil Blackwell Ltd, 1986. Print.

Colvin, H.M., General Editor. (Brown, R. Allen, Lecturer in History, King's College, London; Colvin, H.M., Fellow of St. John's College, Oxford; Taylor, A.J., Chief Inspector of Ancient Monuments, Ministry of Public Building and Works). *The History of the King's Works, Volume One, The Middle Ages.* London: Her Majesty's Stationery Office, 1963. Print.

Dunlop, Eileen. *Queen Margaret of Scotland.* Edinburgh: NMS Enterprises, Limited, 2011. Print

Frantzen, Allen J., General Editor. *Food, Eating and Identity in Early Medieval England.* Woodbridge: The Boydell Press, 2014. Print.

Hefferman, Thomas J., and Matter, E. Ann, Editors. *The Liturgy* ~~o~~ ~~... ....~~*ieval Church, Second Edition.* Kalamazoo: Medieval Institute ~~Print.~~

~~...~~ *Middle Ages: from the Seventh* ~~...~~ *Wimmer, Edited by* ~~...~~ ity of Notre Dame

~~...~~ *Admonitions to His* https://hungarytoday.

~~...~~ *ueen of the Scots: A Life* ~~...~~ sity: Palgrave MacMillan,

~~...~~ *in the Middle Ages.* Oxford:

~~...~~ *eval Travellers.* New York – London: W.W. Nor~~t...~~ ~~P~~rint.

Lynch, Michael; Spearman, Michael; Stell, Geoffrey, Editors. *The Scottish Medieval Town.* Edinburgh: John MacDonald Publishers, 1998. Print.

McKitterick, Rosamond. *Atlas of the Medieval World.* Oxford: University Press, 2004. Print.

Meconi, Honey, Editor. *Medieval Music: The Library of Essays on Music Performance Practice.* New York: University of Rochester, 2011. Print.

Miller, Joseph M., Editor. (Presser, Michael H., and Benson, Thomas W.) *Readings in Medieval Rhetoric: The Etymologies, II. 1 – 15, Concerning Rhetoric.* (Translated by Cerino, Dorothy V.) Bloomington and London: Indiana University Press, 1973. Print.

Murray, H.J.R. *A History of Chess.* Oxford: At the Clarendon Press, 1913. Print.

Monks moved to Pécsvárad
(Zengö Mountain)
distance to Nadasd
11.9 km / 7 miles
1st Benedictines may have
moved in with secular
priests of Pécs Cathedral

Owen, Helen L. *When Did the Catholic Church Decide Priests Should Be Celibate?* The George Washington University, Columbian College of Arts and Sciences. October, 2001. http://historynewsnetwork.org/article/696#sthash.KR6LV107.dpuf

Ritchie, R.L. Graeme. *Normans in Scotland.* Edinburgh: Edinburgh University Presses, 1954. Print.

Robinson, Katelyn. *The Anchoress and the Heart's Nose: The Importance of Smell to Medieval Women Religious.* From "Magistra – A Journal of Women's Spirituality in History," Editor, Judith Sutera, OSB. Volume 19, Number 2. Atchison, Kansas: publications/magistra.html, Winter, 2013. Print.

Ronay, Gabriel. *The Lost King of England: The East European Adventures.* Rochester, NY: Boydell Press, 1989. Print.

Rushforth, Rebecca. *St. Margaret's Gospel-book: The Favourite Book of an eleventh-century Queen of Scots.* Bodleian Library: University of Oxford, 2007. Print.

Saunders, William P., Reverend. *What is the Origin of the Sign of the Cross?* May 22, 2013.

Catholicstraightanswers.com/what-is-the-origin-of-the-sign-of-the-cross/

Singman, Jeffrey L. *The Middle Ages: Everyday Life in Medieval Europe.* New York: Sterling, 2013. Print.

Staniland, Kay. *Medieval Craftsmen: Embroiderers.* Toronto: University of Toronto Press, 1991. Print.

Stanton, Michael, Translator and Editor. *The Anglo-Saxon Chronicle (11th century).* Routledge, New York: University of Exeter, 1996. Print.

Thurston, Herbert. *Aelfric, Abbot of Eynsham.* The Catholic Encyclopedia. Vol. 1, New York: Robert Appleton company, 1907. 13 Aug. 2019 http://newadvent.org/cathen/0117b.htm

Tortora, Phyllis G. and Eubanks, Keith. *Survey of Historic Costume: A History of Western Dress, Second Edition.* New York: Fairchild Publications. Print

Turgot, Bishop of St. Andrews. *Life of St. Margaret, Queen of Scotland.* (12th century). Forgotten Books, 2012. Print.

Undiscovered Scotland https://www.undiscoveredscotland.co.uk/usbiography/monarchs/malcolmiii.html

Verdon, Jean. Translated by George Holoch. *Travel in the Middle Ages.* Notre Dame, Indiana: University of Notre Dame Press, 2003. Print.

Walker, Ian. *Lords of Alba: The Making of Scotland.* Stroud, Gloucester: The History Press, 2013. Print.

Wood, Michael. *Domesday – A Search for the Roots of England.* New York, Oxford: BBC Books, 1986. Print.